AT THE FIRESIDE
~ VOL. 2 ~

AT THE FIRESIDE
~ VOL. 2 ~

TRUE SOUTHERN AFRICAN STORIES

Roger Webster

SPEARHEAD

The cover is by permission from The Lion Match Company Limited, the owner of the rights in the LION match box label.

Published by Spearhead
An imprint of New Africa Books (Pty) Ltd.
99 Garfield Road
Claremont 7700
South Africa

(021) 674 4136
info@newafricabooks.co.za

First edition, second impression 2003

ISBN: 0-86486-536-8

Proofreading by Richard Rufus-Ellis
Layout and design by Peter Stuckey
Cover design by Toby Newsome
Origination by Fotoplate
Printing and binding by Clyson Printers, 11th Avenue, Maitland

Contents

Foreword

How wonderful to have the opportunity once again to grab a beer, a stick of biltong, my favourite checked blanket and settle down around Roger Webster's campfire. I know that he'll make me guffaw, weep and gasp at his vignettes, and that I'll go to bed much the wiser about why our beautiful country is the way it is and why we love it the way we do. I also know that I'll have been introduced to some unsung heroes, some unknown incidents, some 'skelms', traitors, lovers and adventurers. And I will wonder again why history cannot be imparted in this way in every classroom throughout the land. For some years now Safm's devoted listeners to his weekly "Fireside Chats" have been asking the same question. Like me, they will relish this book.

PATRICIA GLYN
Presenter – Safm 104-107

A positive message

R ecently I was given a copy of a speech made by management consultant Guy Lundy. I was so touched by the content and feel it is so topical, that I would like to take this opportunity to share it with you. I hope you will find Mr Lundy's remarks as inspiring as I did.

'I pledge my allegiance to the flag of the United States of America and to the Republic for which it stands, one Nation under God, indivisible, with Liberty and Justice for all.' Every morning, in schools across America, classes come to a halt, as the Pledge of Allegiance is related over the loudspeaker system. Every student stands up and repeats those words. Amazing how such brainwashing is allowed in the land of the free. But perhaps it is not so strange after all! Americans are proud of their nationhood. No matter how big their problems and heaven knows they have a lot of them, they will spend hours telling you, and anybody else who will listen, how fantastic their country is. And, in fact, how America is better than anywhere else in the entire world.

What a contrast this is to the tenor of remarks made by South Africans overseas. These people who gladly put the new South African flag on their cars and support cottage industries importing biltong and Niknaks to munch on as they cheer the Springboks at Twickenham. They are the ones who will spend hours telling anyone who will listen just how awful it is in South Africa, how lucky they are to be in

London and how they are never going back because the country's such a mess! I suppose they are trying to comfort themselves for being holed up in their dingy London apartments under grey London skies, whilst their friends and families enjoy the sunshine and beaches back home!

Yet when I returned to South Africa, instead of being greeted with smiling faces, I was disappointed to find the same pervasive attitude among some South Africans right here at home. People were amazed that I had returned with my French wife. Yet, the reason for my homecoming was perfectly obvious.

Yes, we have our problems, but so does everyone elsewhere. Sure, the rand is down the tubes, but if you look closely enough, just about every other emerging country has suffered the same fate, including, by the way, Australia and New Zealand. Aren't we lucky that we are not living in Argentina where there is a truly massive currency crisis! Sure, a despot runs Zimbabwe, but boy, am I glad I'm not living in Afghanistan. Yes, we have Aids, but we also have an army of people trying to find a cure.

We do have corruption and so do the Americans. Why must we be so hard upon ourselves? In many ways we are far better off in South Africa now than we have been at anytime in our history. People are being educated and housed at a phenomenal rate. We have the world's cheapest electricity. Inflation is the lowest it has ever been in my lifetime! We have economic growth and development everywhere you look. We have so much going for us. So let's concentrate on the positives that surround us everyday – the people, the sunshine, the beauty and the consistent progress being made. Constantly criticising our country harms our own feelings of happiness and well-being as well as the country that deep down in your heart you know you love.

Let's not run down South Africa. Let us all become ambassadors for our country and point out just how far we've come and just how much further we still intend going. How people need to watch out for us on the world arena! Invite them to come and see for themselves and share in the progress.

I have devised my own pledge of allegiance to South Africa. It goes like this:

> I pledge allegiance to the flag of the Republic of South Africa and to the interesting people, places and idiosyncrasies for which it stands, one Nation with several religions, languages and cultures, still indivisible, proud of its freedom, justice, integrity and progress for all.

This is my pledge to my home, to our home, and I am determined to help others discover our strengths.

Here are some facts about our lovely country:

- When Nelson Mandela was inaugurated in 1994, South Africa was insolvent. Today, the deficit is negligible, one of only a handful of countries in such a position. We've had single digit inflation since 1993, following twenty years of double-digit inflation.
- Mortgage rates are the lowest in 22 years and South Africa is today one of only twelve countries where you can drink water from a tap. The quality of our water is the third best in the world.
- Let's go back sixteen years to 1986. A state of emergency had been declared. White men did two years compulsory military service. Some 64 184 black people were removed from so-called white areas. Roughly 3 989 people were detained without trial.
- Our economic growth rate was 0,7%. Today it is 3%.
- Sixty-four countries had instituted a sports boycott against South Africa! Yet, as I speak, we are welcomed into the World Cup and the Welsh play rugby against us in the Free State!
- South African wines win international awards every year. We have the longest wine route in the world.
- Nelson Mandela, our favourite son, is an international icon of forgiveness, tolerance and humanity.
- The Kruger National Park, boasting an innovative management, is the most profitable park anywhere in the world.
- South African Breweries has become one of the biggest in the world and produces over 50% of China's beer.

- Magnificent highways; warm, friendly, vibrant people; the world's most progressive constitution; the invention of kreepy kraulies, biltong and Mrs Ball's chutney.
- The world's best looking population.

South Africans have almost forgotten the Caspirs and guns of the past. It's paradise now in comparison.

Thank you, Guy Lundy, for reminding us all so clearly of who we are, what we really have and what a great Nation we are developing into.

Gquma and the Abelungu

For many years now, various books on South African history have made reference to the 'Abelungu', a race of people who lived on the Pondoland coast, whose origins were purported to have been the result of a marriage between a shipwrecked white woman and a local chief. Books, unfortunately, refer only fleetingly to the subject. But now at last I have been able to unearth a full version of the story.

To all the wonderful people of Port Edward who preserve and document the flora and protect the magnificent natural forest areas and still find time to unravel the history of their lovely region and preserve it – people like Joe Arkel and Dave and Nan Watson – I dedicate this story.

It was a certain W.C. Scully who first recorded the story many, many years ago. He was out fishing with his friend, Nqalate. They had caught some fine kabeljou. Scully was cleaning the fish whilst Nqalate was making a fire, for many black people hate to touch fish which they regard as water snakes. Nqalate bent down to blow the fire, then pulled away and sneezed. 'Gquma ndincede!' he exclaimed. This Scully felt was rather peculiar for, being fluent in Xhosa, he knew that 'gquma' meant 'a roar' like the roar of a lion or the roar of the sea and that 'ndincede' meant 'help me'. Over the braai he questioned Nqalate.

'Gquma whom I evoked,' Nqalate replied, 'is not the roar of the sea, but a woman of your race, who lived many years ago, and whom we, the Tshomane people look upon as the head of our tribe. You will notice that whenever a Tshomane sneezes, he calls on Gquma.'

5

'Gquma,' Nqalate continued, 'was a white woman who came out of the sea when she was a child. She married our great chief Ndepa and together they ruled our tribe. She was the great-great grandmother of our chief Dalasile who died last year'.

Nqalate's account continued. One autumn morning many, many years ago, members of the Tshomane clan who were living in the area to the north-east of the mouth of the Umtati River, were greeted by an astonishing sight. The wind had been blowing strongly from the south-east for a few days and the sea was running very high. Just beyond the furthest line of the breakers lay this immense 'thing', rolling helplessly about in the breakers in the ocean swells. The thing looked like a great ocean fish, such as on rare occasions had been stranded in the neighbourhood. But it had a flat top from which stumps, like tree trunks, protruded. Long strings with immense mats were hanging over the sides and trailing in the water. And, as the rolling brought the flat top into view, creatures resembling human beings could be seen running about.

Not even the oldest members of the tribe had ever seen such an object and they gathered on the shore in amazement. Faint cries repeated at intervals pierced the booming of the surf and a white fabric swelling outwards as it rose was seen on the tallest of the protruding stumps. All day long the monster lay wallowing, impelled shoreward by the swell, slowly being sucked southwards by the current toward the big black rocks at the heads. The Tshomane people slowly followed along the shore towards the rocks. Just after sundown it struck with a crashing thud and thereupon, a long wail of agony arose from the people on it. Then it reeled over somewhat and appeared to start to melt into the sea.

By the time night fell, strange objects, which the people feared to touch, began to be washed up as the people retired to their homes to talk long into the night about these unbelievable happenings.

At the first streak of dawn the people began to re-assemble on the beach. The monster was no longer to be seen, but the entire area was strewn with strange objects and, as the sun rose, the people gathered sufficient confidence to examine the debris. Then a shout went up and people ran to a spot in a wide cleft in the black reef with gleaming white sand. A strange object had been found!

Huddled against a rock on the side of the cleft lay a child. A little white girl with long yellow hair. She was clad in a light garment of a texture unknown to the people. They gazed in astonishment at this strange creature cast up by the sea. At length she opened her eyes. They were the colour of the sky, a feature never previously seen by the inhabitants. Eventually an old man, Gambushe, head councillor to Chief Sango, stepped forward and lifted the little girl into his arms. She was deathly cold but when she felt the warmth of the old man, she flung her arms around his neck, and nestled her face against his shoulder, completely without dread.

And so fate placed a small white girl of about seven years of age in the care of the Tshomane people; and she came to be perceived as a gift from the sea.

Gambushe's kraal was situated behind the sand dunes and he carried the child back to his home. Chief Sango had in the meanwhile issued a decree, stating that everything that had been deposited on the beach was to be carried to his kraal and that nobody was to loot a single thing. This was an era in which the chief's word was akin to that of God and no-one dared disobey. Every item found on the beach was carried by the men, women and children up the long sinuous sandy footpath, across the five miles to the Chief's homestead.

In the afternoon dead bodies began to roll in with the curling surf and the white, bearded faces of the drowned men, most with wide-eyed looks of horror on their faces, struck new terror in the Tshomane people. Black people traditionally shrink in abhorrence from touching a dead body and the course of the afternoon saw the area become cluttered with the dead.

The people sent word to the Chief for instructions and retired terror-stricken to their homes. The next morning the Chief, accompanied by his traditional healers, came down to examine the scene. He called a meeting of the whole tribe for the following day. The complete council, elders and all, came to a unanimous decision. The monster that had died amongst the rocks in the white water was one of the creatures of the sea, sent to bear the little white child to the land of the Tshomane. When she was old enough, she would become the wife of Ndepa, the twelve-year old next in line to the chieftainship. She was the daughter of the mighty ones who dwelt in the sea, her sea-nature clearly revealed by her long hair that resembled seaweed. All the dead people strewn on the beach had been her servants who had now been destroyed for she no longer had need of them. The Chief then gave the order that all the objects washed up on the beach were to be carefully preserved for the use of the white child. And as she had come to the land of the Tshomane when the seas were raging, she was to be named Gquma – roar of the sea.

And so the yellow-haired child was revered as a gift from the gods and all the boxes and objects strewn along the beach were safely collected. Two big huts were constructed to house her possessions.

On an occasion some time later, one of the boxes was opened and the child caught sight of a pair of hairbrushes and a mirror. She immediately seized them and then burst into tears. Later she was seen looking into the mirror as she brushed her hair, tears streaming down her pretty face. For a long time after this she would spend time combing her hair, gently singing and pointing at herself, saying 'Bessie, me Bessie'. But her name Gquma stuck and she quickly learnt the language of the tribe.

Soon afterwards, the Chief donated two pure white cattle to Gquma, which were kept at Gambushe's homestead. Very soon, all the white cattle born to the tribe were donated to her and called Gquma's cattle and her herd grew in great numbers. When she reached womanhood Gquma married Ndepa. But the wedding did not follow the traditional pattern. Gquma placed herself and her maidens at the cleft of the big rocks where she had been found and Ndepa asked permission of the ocean to take her hand in marriage. The full tribe was present on the very solemn occasion. Ndepa became the chief of the Tshomane and Gquma bore him two sons, the elder of whom was called Begala, and a daughter called Bessie.

Gquma lived a happy married life for another eighteen years and finally was struck down by a terrible sickness. On her deathbed she asked to be taken down to the sea and called for Bessie. 'That is where your mother came from,' she told Bessie as she pointed out to sea, and then quietly passed away. She was buried at sea by the Tshomane people. And it is said that on the day after her burial there were hundreds of fish washed up on the shoreline.

The story of Gquma was passed from generation to generation and travelling through the mists of time it has become the tale that I have now related.

Cape Town's gold rush

O f all the historical stories I sift through and recount, the gold rush ones are among my very favourites. From the far corners of the globe – California's 49ers, the Kalgoorlies and Wedderburn in Australia, to our very own Prince Albert Road, Milkwood near Knysna, Melmani, Pilgrim's Rest, Lydenburg and the Witwatersrand – come new gold rush stories. And they have one important ingredient in common – greed.

When told of a new discovery of gold people seem to become blinded to everything else. All reasoning goes out the window. They sell up everything to become part of a quest for possible untold wealth. Look at the Yukon in the north-west of Canada during the 1890s when prospectors suffered temperatures of –40° searching for the 'muck' called gold. Many set out on this path of madness and few returned with destiny having favoured them with fame and fortune.

Pieter Jacob Marais was a prospector from South Africa who had experienced both the Californian and Australian gold rushes with very little to show for his efforts. He returned to his beloved Table Mountain, but it was not too long before he was off again on a trek that was to land him a pioneering role in South African history.

The Volksraad in the Transvaal gave him permission to prospect, with the promise of £5 000 reward, along with a position as mine manager, should he find payable gold deposits. Marais did manage to find gold, some of it in the Jukskei River, just north of the Witwatersrand outcrop, but not in payable quantities; and a sadder but wiser Marais was back in Cape Town in 1855. That was the fate of the first registered prospector of the Transvaal.

The following year, 1856, saw a gold rush in Cape Town, the first and last ever experienced in the Mother City. It took place on the slopes of Table Mountain in Platteklip Gorge, not far from the cave where Lieutenant-General R. J. Gordon had in the previous century entranced William Hickley and his friends with 'celestial music' and a breakfast feast.

Cape Town's citizens streamed up the stony gorge armed with picks and shovels, sieves and homemade sluice boxes. Nobody was going to miss out on this wonderful opportunity. If a piece of gold-bearing ore had been found in Platteklip Gorge by a servant working for Mr Salem, the local auctioneer, surely there was a chance to find more.

On entering the gorge the prospectors found that Mr Salem had set up a refreshment base next to the stream. He welcomed them with the ready patter characteristic of the auctioneer's art. His ale, wine and spirits, along with his sandwiches, sold extremely well, at prices almost double the town price. Fossicking around in the mountains is hot and hard work and the citizens were only too happy to pay these prices.

For five whole days the people of Cape Town and surrounding areas streamed up that mountain, but to no avail. Nobody found the slightest trace of gold while Mr Salem did a roaring trade at the foot of the gorge.

Eventually the truth of the matter emerged. Sure the gold that Mr Salem's servant had shown to everybody was real. It had come from Australia. Mr Salem had bought it and kept it ever since the events in Cape Town surrounding the boycott of the convict ship, the *Neptune*. He had bided his time for an opportunity to get his own back on the town as Mr Salem, you see, was an ex-convict from Van Diemen's Land.

Of course, after that fiasco, the auctioneer did not stay long in Cape Town. Capetonians, on the other hand, wiped away the dust and dreams of instant wealth and went back to their everyday lives, trusting that their embarrassment would fade with the passage of time.

Huberta the Hippo

A most intriguing South African story concerns the travels of a certain hippopotamus. Her journey was to last three years during which she would become the most famous traveller of her time. Still today, some 70 years on, her story continues to captivate both young and old.

Her birthplace was probably in the northern regions of KwaZulu-Natal, beyond the Lake St. Lucia district. Nobody knows why the yearning for travel overcame this young female hippo, as she wallowed in the slushy waters of Lake St. Lucia. All we do know is that early in 1928 she first came to the notice of the public when newspapers began publishing a record of her journey southwards. Initially the papers named the hippo Bill, then the more dignified name of Hubert, until it was discovered that the hippo was actually a female; and her name was changed to Huberta which then stuck.

The international press, fascinated by her slow and sometimes belaboured journey south, took up the story, and she became a celebrity. She was spotted at the present day Richards Bay on the banks of the Umhlatuzi River in November of 1928. Ever southwards she continued, past Mtunzini, the mouth of the Tugela and at New Gelderland, a huge crowd gathered next to the railway line, trying desperately to catch a glimpse of the now famous animal. She very quickly became known as 'South Africa's national pet' and 'The Union's most famous tourist'. The international press lapped it all up and crowd after crowd of curious sightseers assembled along the way to catch sight of Huberta.

Some of the people in the crowds were cruel and, as she trekked onwards, they hurled stones, bottles and sticks at her, in order to force her from the hiding places that she had sought refuge in. She reached Durban North in March of 1929 with the crowds waiting in anticipation. In the following month, she lolloped into Durban, some 250 kilometres distant from her starting place.

It was at this point that legends about her started forming. When she entered Annerley, a small village on the coast south of Durban, the local Hindi community apparently deified her. According to contemporary accounts, she was proclaimed 'Protector of the Poor' during a service in the local temple. Some Zulu people, it is said, declared that Huberta was the reincarnation of the great warrior King Shaka returning to his land. The Mpondo, further down the coast, thought her to be the spirit of a famous traditional healer, who was descended from a survivor of the wreck of the *Grosvenor*. Xhosa people, still further south, believed that the animal was the spirit of a great chief such as Sandile or Hintsa, who had returned, at last, to seek justice for his people.

Whatever the beliefs, she was watched, loved and revered by the entire world! In January 1930 she had reached Port St. Johns on the Transkei coast and in December of that year, she was spotted along the banks of the Buffalo River, near East London, almost 1 000 kilometres away from the starting point of her epic journey. Still she persevered southwards, until she reached the Keiskamma River, where she turned right, starting to head upstream and, to this day, nobody can tell you why.

On the morning of 24 April 1930, on an isolated farm on the banks of the Keiskamma River, a certain elderly granny was working away in her kitchen, with her six-year old grandson. She heard two shots ring out. 'Oh, my God,' cried out the granny, 'I hope that wasn't the Hippo!' But it was. Huberta had plunged into the river and was running along the bottom. Under the water she ran as fast as her legs could carry her. Two neighbouring farmers were in pursuit. She surfaced about 500 metres upstream and then a hail of bullets was pumped into her skull. Huberta was no more!

A huge public outcry followed. A nation hung its head in shame and the international community was stunned by the news that Huberta's life had been so needlessly snuffed out. The killing was discussed in parliament and the police were instructed to investigate the matter. The farmers eventually appeared in court on the charge of killing 'royal game'. They were found guilty and each fined £25, but of what use was that to a nation that had lost its favourite pet.

Captain G. C. Shortridge of the Amathole Museum in King William's Town took possession of the remains and had the carcass skinned. Huberta was sent to England for mounting. Sympathy cards, donations, and wreaths of flowers were sent in memory of Huberta. Almost all the associated costs for the project were met by the *Cape Mercury*'s 'Huberta's Shilling Fund', supported by people from all over South Africa.

Huberta's final home is near the entrance of the Natural History building in the Amathole Museum. It is one of the finest museums in our country and, under the excellent directorship of Mr Lloyd Wingate and curatorship of Stephanie, the memory of Huberta will live on for generations to come. Pop in there one day; it is well worth the effort.

Bvenkenya – 'The one who swaggers as he walks'

S tephanus Cecil Barnard, born in Knysna on 19 September 1886, was revered by many Africans and became a legend in his lifetime. His African name 'Bvenkenya' means 'The one who swaggers as he walks'.

He grew up in Knysna and later moved with his parents to a farm near the present-day town of Schweizer-Reneke, on the western flank of Paul Kruger's Transvaal. The family worked hard and the farm prospered until 1896, when disaster struck in the form of the rinderpest. Old man Barnard sat down beside his last dying ox and wept, as he saw the days, weeks and years of hard physical toil disappear like rain puddles in the hot Transvaal sun.

Three years later, Barnard senior, with his four older boys, left to fight in the Anglo-Boer War, leaving Mrs Barnard with the five younger children to eke out what existence they could. Stephanus was the oldest of the children remaining on the farm. Not long afterwards the heavy toil and the ever-present worry of destitution and starvation began to take its toll on Mrs Barnard. As the war drew to a close, she sickened and died, leaving the fifteen-year old Stephanus as acting head of the family. Running the farm by himself, with the help of only his four younger brothers and sisters, proved impossible. So he took whatever odd jobs the neighbourhood could offer.

At the end of that terrible war, which brought such devastation to the region, his father and elder brothers returned. A few years later, in April of 1906, with a scrappy education and no money, Stephanus left home in search of fortune. He had never forgotten the Knysna forest elephants of his youth and the stories of elephant mystery, romance and adventure with which his father had regaled him each night. By 1910 Stephanus had succeeded in purchasing clothing, food, camp gear, a wagon, ten donkeys and a couple of good guns. In the winter of that year he, like so many others before him, took the Great North Road out of Pretoria on the first stage of adventure into the interior.

As time passed, he found his way to a place known as 'Crook's Corner'. It is at this spot that Zimbabwe, Mozambique and South Africa meet, on the north-eastern boundary of what is today the Kruger National Park. As its name suggests, here was the meeting place of all sorts of nefarious people – cattle rustlers, murderers and people generally on the run from the law.

There was a good bush telegraph system in operation at that time and warnings of the imminent arrival of policemen from South Africa were received in good time. The crooks of 'Crook's Corner' were suitably prepared and simply moved the boundary beacon! They were safe as they were not strictly speaking in South Africa but in Mozambique. When a fresh round of authorities arrived, the crooks had 'moved to Zimbabwe' and so the game went on with the police constantly thwarted.

Over the years Stephanus became an elephant and ivory trader of considerable fame and the nickname, Bvenkenya, was attached to him. Stories of his life were recounted, mixed with interesting folklore and myths of the tribes deep in the South African and Mozambique bush. Stories of virgin sacrifices to the crocodile, God of the Lake, of hippos, lion and elephant, along with very touching human dramas, abounded.

A tale is told of how, for the entire duration of his hunting and poaching career, he tried in vain to track down and shoot a particularly huge male elephant, named Dhlulamithi. This wily old pachyderm would always slip out of Bvenkenya's clutches. It became an obsession, as happens when something continues to elude one. Slipping out of the

16

corner of one's eye or gliding through one's consciousness during the betwixt times, it starts to take on a life of its own.

Such was Bvenkenya's relationship with Dhlulamithi. When he eventually managed to corner the animal and had the elephant firmly fixed in his sights down the barrel of a gun, a very strange feeling came over him. It was as if he was spellbound. He hesitated. He could not pull the trigger. Dhlulamithi slowly turned to face the moment of his death, looking Bvenkenya straight in the eyes. Bvenkenya could not shake off the strange feeling. He slowly lowered his rifle, stood upright (which, if you know elephants, is not a clever thing to do!) and said to the elephant, 'Go – go to your cows, and may you have many strong sons that will follow in your footsteps.' Bvenkenya turned his back on the elephant and started to walk away. The elephant did not charge; it stood there and watched him disappear into the dense African bush.

It is said that after this experience Bvenkenya never hunted elephants again. He returned to his farm just outside Geysdorp in the Western Transvaal. He married Maria Badenhorst and there together they raised four sons and a daughter – just as he had wished for Dhlulamithi.

Bvenkenya died on 2 June 1962. In true family fashion his son Izak Barnard started the earliest safari tour company in southern Africa, Penduka, which means 'turn round' or 'return'. In turn the son and grandsons of Izak Barnard became legends amongst the Bushmen in the Kalahari Desert. Outside a small Botswana town by the name of Malepolole, there is a clan of Bushmen who treat the Barnard family like their own.

I sincerely hope that the legacy of Bvenkenya and his family will continue for generations to come and that somebody will, eventually, make a film of this family's epic-like story.

A tribute to loyalty and courage

Wednesday, 22 May 2002, was a terribly sad day for southern Africa. It saw the passing of one of our greatest heroines, Lady Ruth Khama of Botswana.

Ruth Williams was born to a middleclass family in Blackheath in south-east London. She met Seretse Khama in 1948 and the couple fell in love, but it was not a good time for a love such as theirs. Her family opposed the relationship and Tshekedi, Seretse's uncle and Bamangwato Regent, was against him marrying a white woman from a country so vastly different from their own.

In addition, the National Party had come into power in South Africa and a mixed marriage of an important chief to a white, English-speaking woman on the borders of South Africa did not form a part of their apartheid design. On the other side of the ocean Britain was debt-ridden and dependent on South Africa as a source of strategic minerals. Roughly ninety percent of the world's uranium came from South Africa and London handled all the country's gold. Britain was therefore reluctant to annoy the white government.

Despite external pressures, Ruth and Seretse would not be swayed. Seretse ignored his uncle's wishes and Ruth, as a result, was cast out from her family home. As soon as their marriage plans became known the British Government and the London Missionary Society decided to intervene. Officials informed the local priest that when the ceremony was to take place and reach the stage where opposition to the marriage could be expressed, they would declare the possibility that Setetse was already married – and in that way disrupt the proceedings. Ruth was devastated.

As a result of the dispute, the parish priest was forced to try to obtain permission from the Bishop of London but, unfortunately, the Foreign Office had reached the Bishop first. By the time Ruth and Seretse had secured an interview, their fate had already been sealed. Permission for the marriage was denied. Ruth was heartbroken and her dreams for a beautiful wedding in her local church to the man she so completely loved, lay shattered.

The couple had to marry in a registry office. Afterwards they left England to settle with his people, the Bamangwato, in Serowe, Botswana, where the local elders called the biggest kgotla or tribal meeting ever. After many hours of debate, Seretse rose and said, 'All those who will not accept my wife, please stand up.' Forty people were counted. 'Now, all those who will accept my wife, please stand up.' Six thousand people rose to their feet and applauded him for ten minutes. The tribe had spoken, but the British government continued its machinations. When Seretse returned to London for talks, he was informed that he was banned from Bechuanaland for five years and, after the Tories returned to power, the five-year term was changed to 'indefinitely'.

The couple remained in England and Seretse continued his legal studies. In 1956 he renounced his claim to the chieftainship and it was only then that the British government allowed the couple to return as 'private parties', whereupon Seretse set about forming the Democratic Party of Botswana.

In 1966 Britain granted independence to Bechuanaland and in the elections that followed the Party won a landslide victory. Seretse became the first Prime Minister of a now free country called the Republic of Botswana. Needless to say, the Bamangwato had long ago accepted him as their legitimate chief and people had grown to know and to love 'The Queen', as they called Ruth. In the same year Seretse was knighted by Queen Elizabeth II for the benefits his rule had brought.

Sir Seretse Khama passed away in 1980 at the age of 59, leaving behind his beloved Ruth and their four children. A few people speculated at the time that Lady Khama would retire to England. But clearly they had no inkling of the woman's mettle. She remained at home with her people.

Lady Khama became known as 'Mohumagadi Mma Kgosi' (Mother of the Chief) and as the Queen Mother, when her eldest son Ian took over as Chief of the Bamangwato people. Today the same son, Lieutenant-General Ian Khama, is Vice-President of Botswana.

It is important to know and understand the background of the Khama family who continue to play a key role in the southern African region. As for the late Queen Mother of Botswana, Lady Ruth Khama, seldom has such love and devotion been shown to a man and his people, in the face of such adversity.

ROBALA KA KHUTSO NKGONO – Rest in peace, granny.

Sarah Baartman

I t is very heartening to see ordinary South Africans taking an interest in the history of our country. They are starting to question the old biased stories and examine the past with new perspectives. This and this alone will eventually break down the enormous barriers and fill those voids that the old kind of history-telling created.

The story of Sarah Baartman is a case in point. It is also a very topical one as her remains have only recently been returned to South Africa and buried in her country of birth.

We know quite a lot about Sarah's life but what we hardly have any record of, and what we can only imagine, is the immense personal pain and suffering that this young woman underwent during the years she was a virtual slave on foreign shores. Her fate was not dissimilar to the two Inuits, who, on being captured by Captain Frobischer off the coast of Baffin Land, were locked up in a cabin. On the journey to England the Inuits were monitored on a rotational basis by the crew, to confirm the gross speculation that they might 'mate' as animals!

'Saartjie' as she was known until recently, was Khoekhoe. It is believed that she was born near the Gamtoos River in the Eastern Cape. She left her home as a young teenager. In March 1810 she was living near Cape Town when a ship's surgeon, Alexander Dunlop, met her. She was enticed with promises of fame and fortune to board his ship and accompany him to London. He promised that within two years he would make them both rich, for one of Sarah's striking characteristics, at least as far as Europeans were concerned, were her large buttocks or steatopygia, which is the result of fatty tissue around the buttocks.

Written into Sarah's contract was a clause in which she agreed 'to be viewed by the public of England and Ireland just as she was'. Like so many girls who are attracted to the bright lights, she was lured into the life of what effectively was a stripper and later a prostitute.

She was displayed at the home of Dunlop's partner, Hendrick Caesar, in York Street, Picadilly, London, to anyone who would pay the entrance fee and, in time, became known as 'The Hottentot Venus'. Led onto the low stage like an animal by her keeper, Sarah was exhibited, wearing only the scantiest of clothing. Her keeper gave her orders in Dutch, instructing her to 'sit, stand and turn around' and generally walking her around for the audience's entertainment. It was noted that, on a number of occasions, she was reluctant to obey and that the keeper had to threaten her. At one performance, it is said, a Dutch-speaking man who was in the audience tried to ask her questions, but Sarah's keeper immediately drowned out her replies and then led her weeping off the stage.

This was the period of the growing Anti-Slavery movement in Britain and Dunlop therefore quickly drew up a new contract. It was dated 20 October 1810 and covered a period of five years retrospective from the date on which Sarah had been removed from the Cape Colony. The contract stated the following conditions. She was employed as a domestic servant and for this job she would be paid twelve guineas a year. She agreed to exhibit herself in public in the nude. And, finally, she would be free to return to the Cape after the five-year contract period. Dunlop's move was none to soon, for the Attorney-General intended taking action against him, based on affidavits supplied to the State.

The case was heard on 24 November but the new contract proved to be watertight. A year after this celebrated case, on 7 December 1811, Sarah was baptised by the Rev. Joshua Brookes at the Parish Church of Christ in Manchester, with permission of the Lord Bishop of Chester.

In September 1814 Sarah was taken to Paris and fell under the control of a keeper of wild animals. She was exhibited again to all who were willing to pay three francs. She became an even greater attraction in the French capital than she had been in London. A prurient public flocked to see her and buy her portrait and she was featured in satirical cartoons. In November 1814, a one-act farce, 'The Hottentot Venus, or the Hatred to French Women', began a long and popular run at the Vaudeville Theatre in Paris. In March the following year, a commission of biologists and physiologists, consisting of Baron George Cuvier, Geoffroy St Hilaire and Henri de Blainville, examined Sarah over a three-day period.

In a back street of Paris on New Year's Day in 1816, Sarah died of an unknown disease, without ever again seeing the beloved home that she had left six years earlier.

But a further indignity was heaped on her after her death. Her body was cast and then dissected. Her brain, genitalia and full skeleton were preserved and placed on public display in the Musee de l'Homme in Paris and her remains kept on display there until 1974. Now, at last, after a period of 189 years, she has made the return journey she so desperately wanted to do. Sarah Baartman is coming home to her people.

Sammy Marks

espite escaping conscription into the army, the young Sammy Marks was left with an abiding hatred of Tsarist Russia. In 1861 before he turned eighteen, Sammy had left Russia and set sail for Hull, with a consignment of Russian horses, bound for the industrial city of Sheffield in northern England.

Sheffield society was undergoing radical change and expansion as it developed into the cradle of the English steel industry. The town was attracting thousands of newcomers. Sammy was welcomed to his new refuge by a kinsman who ran a jewellery shop and readily supplied him with the seed money to set up a peddler's business. At the same time Sammy found lodgings with a prominent member of the Jewish community, Tobias Guttmann, a jeweller, hawker and cutler, who became the young man's mentor.

Guttmann advised the young man to sail for South Africa to try his luck on those distant shores. He agreed to pay for Sammy's passage to Cape Town and also presented him with a large case of knives, the sum total of the young man's capital. Perhaps it was his youthful experiences in industrial England that later provided Sammy Marks with the inspiration to establish, among a host of other companies, a Transvaal version of Sheffield, viz. the large steelworks at Vereeniging. Who knows?

Marks arrived at the Cape which was also undergoing important historical change. The year before, in 1867, a large diamond, the 'Eureka', had been discovered on a remote farm in the northern area of the colony and this was followed within a year by the discovery of the 'Star of South Africa' diamond. These events led to the beginnings of a mineral industry that was to revolutionise the sub-continent.

Marks stayed initially in Cape Town. He hawked his stock of knives around Cape Town and made a pleasant profit, reinvesting the profit in goods, which he again peddled in the suburbs of Cape Town. His cousin, Isaac Lewis, joined him, and the partnership prospered. Soon they had accumulated sufficient cash to buy a horse and cart and then another. With goods obtained on credit from Cape Town's wholesale merchants, they extended their 'smousing' into the Boland, Cape Town's then rural hinterland.

In July 1871 news came of a discovery of a major diamond pipe and this set off a frenzied rush. The partners loaded their two carts with goods and immediately set off. But long before they had reached their destination, they had sold every article to the poorly equipped hopefuls making their way to the diamond fields. They turned back to Cape Town, restocked the carts, taking with them this time a prefabricated wooden shop. Arriving at the diggings, they sold off a cart and a horse and opened shop. Goods were in short supply and they made a handsome profit. Payments were made mostly in diamonds and Lewis and Marks soon found that dealing in diamonds was more profitable than trading in general goods.

Lewis and Marks rapidly established a reputation for square dealing which placed them head and shoulders above the dubious types known as 'kopje wallopers' and the petty diamond buyers, who scuttled around the claims, gulling credulous diggers.

Within a very short space of time, Lewis and Marks, along with a handful of diamond merchants, came to dominate the local trade, acting as intermediaries between Kimberley and the great diamond centres of Europe. In a little corrugated iron office, situated in the new main street between the Albion Bar and the Diggers Arms, stones were brought in for sale. Here the partners made their selections to ship off to merchants in London, Amsterdam and elsewhere. Such were the humble beginnings of Sammy Mark's enormously successful career.

Anthony Trollope, a novelist visiting Kimberley in October 1877, found the area 'a most detestable place'. He complained: 'Temperatures soared to 50° in the sun, the landscape was drought stricken and totally bare. I don't think there was a tree to be seen within five miles of the town.' He continued: 'I doubt whether there was a blade of grass for twenty miles, and everything was a drab brown colour where one gagged on an atmosphere of dust and flies. The dust is so thick that the sufferer fears to remove it lest the raising of it may aggravate the evil, and flies are so numerous that one hardly dares to slaughter them by the ordinary means least the bodies should be noisome.'

But the Marks-Lewis partnership endured those terrible climes and they began to invest heavily in diamond mining, buying their first claims in 1872. The restriction limiting the purchase of claims was removed in 1874 and this opened the way for substantial capital investment. Claim holders fell from 1 600 to just 300 by 1877. Fewer than twenty claim holders controlled over half of the claims, while four businesses, the Lewis and Marks partnership, the Paddon brothers, Jules Porges and J. B. Robinson owned a quarter of the entire mine between them.

The partners, the Paddon brothers and a few others, combined their claims to form the Kimberley Mining Company, one of the earliest mining companies on the fields. By 1879, its capital had increased to £200 000, of which Lewis and Marks held half, and the venture was soon giving a return on capital of over 25%. It was then that Lewis went to England to negotiate their company's merger with claims held by Jules Porges; and a new combined company was floated in Paris, Compagnie Francaise des Mines du Diamantes du Cap.

A joint stock company with a capital of 14 million francs or £560 000, it was the largest mining concern in Africa, representing nearly one quarter of the richest diamond mine on the Cape diamond fields. This was the first South African diamond mining company to be placed before the investing public in Europe and its floatation was an enormous success. By mid-1880 its shares were trading freely at a very high premium.

When Sammy Marks noticed the tensions building up after the Jameson Raid by British-aligned forces, he decided to become active on

26

the diplomatic front. He ran between the two parties trying desperately to avert the ever-growing spectre of war in the Transvaal. He pleaded with President Kruger for a change in attitude and stated on numerous occasions that war with Britain would destroy not only the Transvaal and Orange Free State, but also the very core of the Boer nation. Unfortunately, these wise sentiments fell on deaf ears. The inevitable happened.

After the fall of Bloemfontein, Johannnesburg and Pretoria to the British, Sammy Marks desperately tried to convince the Boer generals that it was useless to continue the war. In a letter addressed to Louis Botha and other Boer Generals, he pleaded: 'I ask you and my other friends, if 10 000 men can possibly hope to prevail against a mighty power like England, backed by her colonies and dependencies, which has at her command almost unlimited funds and numberless men. It is not necessary for me to point to the number of widows and orphans as a result of the war, and to tell you that the number is rapidly increasing, and what will be the end? It is all very well for our brave leaders and men in the field to talk about fighting to the bitter end, but you must not forget the thousands of prisoners who are exiled from their country and have been for months. The longer the war lasts the greater will be the destruction wrought and the consequences will be that when the prisoners are brought back to the country, they will have no houses to receive them. Do you not think as a Man, a General, a Husband, and a Father, you should determine to make the best of things, and prevail upon others to do the same?'

Such was the passion that Sammy had for the Boer people and for his country. But his appeals were in vain. The letter was sent to General Botha's camp, personally delivered to him by the widow of the late General Piet Joubert. And the result – the Boers were incensed!

As the commandos grew increasingly desperate, they attacked Marks's home at Zwartkoppies and stole a number of horses. His wife Bertha was at home, alone and was terrorised by the commando until four in the morning. The incident angered Sammy deeply. Yet he continued to do what he could for the Boers and their cause. Indeed, he initiated the talks on 19 May, which culminated in the Peace of Vereeniging being signed on 31 May 1902.

Sammy also put aside money to get the Boer generals back on their feet. One day as he came out of the bank in Pretoria, he met Koos de la Rey going in. 'What's that large envelope under your arm?' he asked. 'I have business with the bank,' came the reply. 'Please come with me to my office,' Sammy requested. He shut the door and asked to see the contents of De la Rey's envelope. Inside were the title deeds of De la Rey's farms. 'You were going to mortgage them?' Sammy asked. 'I have no choice, it is for my children's education,' came the soft reply. 'Don't be a fool, you will be ruined in a couple of years. I will lend you all that you require, and you can repay me when you can afford it.' This was the kind of generosity Sammy Marks was capable of.

In the post-war boom Marks and Lewis invested heavily in property in the western Transvaal and the Cape. They floated an enormously powerful company, The African & European Investment Company. In 1912 Marks formed the Vereeniging Power Station and then went on to found the South African Iron and Steel Corporation, which was the culmination of a 37 year dream. Although the furnace was small and of an experimental nature, it marked the beginning of steel production made from local highveld ore.

Sammy Marks died of a stomach ailment in Johannesburg on 18 February 1920 at the age of 75. Shops and businesses closed to show their respect. Friends, colleagues and luminaries, including the Prime Minister of South Africa, Jan Smuts, who had been a long-time friend, were present at the graveside in Pretoria. South Africa had lost a visionary and pioneer, and one of its most influential industrialists. A 'haimishe mensch' indeed!

The legendary ivory

Among the many ancient tales and myths that I have come across in Africa, from the Lost City of the Kalahari to the Kruger Millions, nothing has intrigued me more than this story of a mysterious elephant burial place.

When the hunters of old used to gather around the campfires of Africa at night, the talk was sure to turn, sooner or later, to a place that was known as Ivory Valley. This was a great cemetery to which dying elephants, guided by instinct, were said to make their way.

Frederick Selous, Trader Horn, Henry Hartley, Oswold Cotton and many other famous adventurers believed the legend implicitly. The reasons were numerous and the stories enchanting, but the legend of the elephant cemetery in the Kaokoveld has persisted, based mainly upon two facts.

The first is that the Herero people would appear from time to time, carrying heavy loads of valuable ivory tusks – tusks which had obviously not been cut off newly killed elephants. 'We found them in the bush' would be their standard reply. That was their story and they stuck to it. No hunter could ever persuade a Herero to lead him to this apparently endless supply.

The second supposedly indisputable reason that the hunters gave was that apart from the elephants they shot or trapped, they never found elephant remains. Elephants are certainly the easiest animals to spot and the Kaokoveld was teeming with them. Their giant spoor could be seen for miles around the waterholes. Herds, stampeding along the horizon, were regularly seen, but never any dead elephants. It is true that some elephants in the wild live to be a century old, but even then, amongst those enormous herds, there were surely deaths each month? The question the hunters of old asked was where did the dying elephants go?

The solution to the puzzle lay, it was said, in a mysterious valley. When the elephants knew death was upon them, trumpeting the shrill call of finality, they would vanish into the secret valley, where the huge skeletons of their ancestors lay bleached by the blazing African sun.

As far as I know, there has never been a thorough search for the Ivory Valley of the Kaokoveld. In other parts of Africa people have combed tropical forests and bush, quiet lakes and mountain craters to find the elephant sanctuaries. But what lies hidden under the ever-shifting sands in the barren stretch of land in the Kaokoveld, has never really been explored.

Few records were kept about the early exploits of ivory poachers in that then uncharted land. Yet, in times gone by, many bold Boers crossed the Kunene River, returning from the former Portuguese Angola with great loots of ivory.

One Boer recorded how a chief named Oorlog, described as a potentate of mixed ancestry, had captured him. He told how Oorlog (meaning 'war' in Afrikaans) believed that all the elephants in the Kaokoveld belonged to him. The man was taken captive and then a runner sent to the police post on the very edge of the Kaokoveld with the news. He was tried for ivory poaching, declared not guilty, but fined £50 for entering a forbidden territory without a permit. This man swore until the day that he died that Oorlog had told him of the valley of ivory and that no white man would ever learn the secret whereabouts of this most holy place.

Donald Bain, a well-known South African hunter, once camped near a waterhole on the elephant trail in the Kaokoveld. They pitched camp in darkness and did not notice that the tent stood between two elephant paths.

'Just after midnight,' Bain recalled, 'I was raised by the barking of my dogs, and the trumpeting of an elephant. I sat up and saw a mountain on legs coming towards me. Instinctively, I rolled over, expecting to be crushed. For a few seconds, there was pandemonium, the dogs barking, the native bearers shouting and the elephant trumpeting. It had caught its legs in the guy ropes. Mercifully the elephant passed on, crashing through the undergrowth.' Bain then described what he felt was a very eerie experience. 'After all was over, I saw my dog Fritz, standing there shivering from head to foot and yelping for all the world as though someone was beating him.'

The elephants of the Kaokoveld have been protected for many years now and one does not know what changes have been wrought in their ancient patterns of behaviour. Perhaps the cemetery is still in usage? Who can really tell?

Let us conclude with a poem by Cullen Gouldsbury – it may help to convey some sense of that secret place.

Pile upon pile of bleaching bone, and a foul miasmic breath,
With now and again a mighty moan, to break the hush of death –
Sluggish streams, and silver beams, of a silent moon on high –
God forefend, I should meet my end, in the place where elephants die.

The nursemaid of Mrs Lindsay

T he now very famous dairy of private Buck Adams detailing life on the Eastern Frontier of South Africa during the early 1900s, contains a story that shows to what lengths love can drive people. The same story was recorded in the Fort Beaufort Museum and has subsequently been proved to be factual.

A young woman grew up together with her childhood sweetheart in a tiny English village. Ann was expected to marry John Marvell as the two were inseparable – or so it appeared. On no particular day or occasion, John Marvell just simply upped and disappeared, leaving neither a note, nor any explanation as to why or where he was going. Ann was totally mortified!

Being a young woman of strong will, she decided on her own course of action. John had always said that he would like to be a sailor and she was convinced that he had run away to sea. She was determined to find her lover and one day, just like him, Ann quietly slipped away from her village. She had borrowed her brothers' clothes and dressed as a man in order not to attract attention along the way – in those days women did not travel unaccompanied.

Soon afterwards she signed on as an assistant steward and so she began her first trip aboard a sailing vessel. Even if it meant sailing right around the world, she was determined to find John. She enquired at every port of call, but alas, in vain, for John had 'taken the shilling'. He had joined the army, under an assumed name!

Undaunted, Ann continued her searching and in 1842 she obtained a post aboard the S.S. *Abercrombie Robinson*. A sailor's lot in those days was not a comfortable one, the hours were long, the work hard and the accommodation was uncomfortable and cramped. Not to mention the sadistic punishments and the miserable food. A typical daily ration consisted of a pound of mouldy ship-biscuits, three quarters of a pound of salted beef or pork and three quarts of water. Twice a week they received one pound of bully beef and half a pound of bread. The biscuits were usually Liverpool 'pantiles' and harder than the hobs of hell. They had to be banged on the side of the hold before being edible, not so much to soften them as to bang out all the weevils and maggots. The salted meat was generally horsemeat and one could not tell what was more rancid, the salted pork or the butter!

Amidst these primitive conditions, Ann was accepted by her fellow sailors and her gender was never questioned, until, one day, whilst working on the rigging, she slipped and fell on to the deck. It was when she was taken to the doctor that they discovered that she was, in fact, a woman.

Again we see how fate can play such an enormous role in one's life, and in this case it led to the end of Ann's quest. Aboard the *Abercrombie Robinson* was the 91st Regiment, headed for the Cape of Good Hope. After Ann's real identity was discovered, the wife of Lieutenant-General Lindsay, the Commanding Officer of the regiment, took Ann under her wing and employed her as a nursemaid for her children. The *Abercrombie Robinson* docked in Cape Town and the troops and everyone else disembarked. The following evening a gale force wind and storm hit the Cape and the *Abercrombie Robinson* was driven ashore and totally wrecked, leaving the unfortunate Ann with no other choice but to accompany Mrs Lindsay, with the regiment, to the Eastern Frontier outpost, Fort Beaufort. During this time Ann became very close to the Lindsays and eventually confided the story of her love quest to them.

One afternoon, she returned from a walk with the children, clearly in a state of shock, but she refused to divulge what had happened. Eventually, it came out. She had noticed that the sentry on duty outside was none other than John Marvell!

Lieutenant-General Lindsay's assistance was called on and the guard rosters checked but there was nobody by the name John Marvell. The soldier was paraded and, under close questioning, the man known as Mullins broke down and confessed that he was John Marvell. The use of another identity was not an unusual occurrence in those days. Many men, for varying reasons, enlisted under false names. The Colonel then contrived a meeting between the Ann and John. It is difficult to imagine how John felt faced with his childhood sweetheart after all that time and thousands of miles away from his home. A very touching reconciliation, however, took place between the two and once more they plighted their troth, and decided to marry as soon as John had become a sergeant. The Colonel then saw to it that John was promoted and their wedding day was fixed.

On the eve of the wedding, John was returning from Grahamstown. Before him lay the Koonap River, in full spate. He could not bear the thought of any delay and plunged in. He managed fine until halfway across, but then he tired and as he did so he was swept downstream by the relentless floodwaters. His struggles were in vain and he drowned.

Ann was inconsolable. It is said that she nearly died of grief. 'So long in searching and waiting,' she later said, 'so close in presence and time, but, alas, never ever to be.'

It was some years later that she eventually recovered sufficiently to marry Troop Sergeant-Major Samuel Moffat of the Seventh Dragoon Guards. She bore him two sons and a daughter and lived a hard but happy life.

Ann Moffat died in the autumn of 1851 and is buried in an unmarked grave at Peddie, between King William's Town and Grahamstown. Where precisely is not known and I would certainly love one day to pinpoint its exact location.

The springbok migration

In the north-western Cape, far to the north of the Bokkeveldberge, there are little hamlets with lovely names like Bloemhoek, Namies, Aggeneys, Pella and Pofadder, located in the semi-desert, where the Karoo bush grows only about a metre tall.

Some say this dry and harsh land was the creation of an angry God. Yet, it is this very place that was once witness to one of the most spectacular sights in South Africa – the migration of the springbok or 'trekbokken'.

This annual trek was the result of a deep and underlying impulse that led the females to drop their young somewhere far upon the eastern fringe of the desert that extends north and south for several hundred kilometres. This imaginary line is the limit of the rains that fall between April and September. With the rains came the lush green herbage so necessary for the newly-born fawns. For weeks before the main trek started, herds of buck could be seen slowly gathering.

If you stand there today, looking out over the desolate plains, and you allow your eyes to lose focus and your mind to wander, you may just see the huge cloud of dust building up on the horizon. The annual trek has begun, as springbok by the millions start the eastward migration. Their numbers are uncountable, stretching from horizon to horizon, and moving with only one thing in mind – to reach the limit of the rain belt.

It is said that if you had placed a stake in the ground then, it would have taken a medium-sized trek, stretching from horizon to horizon, just under a week to move past this one point.

For the hunters and the trekboers it was a period of great excitement. Every male above the age of ten refurbished his rifle. All sorts of firearms were gathered and flintlocks, more than a century old, hauled out for the occasion. After breakfast, the men moved off in their wagons drawn by teams of oxen towards different points on the trek-line. No horses were taken as, after a day, horses became useless in the dry country, while the oxen could survive the heat and dry, thirsty conditions for a week.

The destination reached, wagons were outspanned and the cattle driven back to town. Every man made himself a makeshift shelter or 'skerm', by pulling up the scrub-bush and laying it in a semi-circle facing the oncoming trek. This became his hiding place. The migrating springbok arrived like lemmings on their way to certain death. The slaughter commenced. There was no art in shooting the animals for they had only one thing in mind – to reach the rain belt. As buck after buck was brought down, the surrounding ones scattered, only to fall into the view of a neighbouring 'skerm' and be killed. When the sun reached its height at noon, the springbok stopped to rest and in the confused melée that followed there was death all around. In the late afternoon servants were brought to the scene of great slaughter to gather the dead.

The unbounded desert spaces held little sanctuary for the springbok. Hyenas and jackals hung on the outskirts of their trek and the vultures wheeled above, ready to tear out the eyes of the less vigorous lagging behind. Sportsman and pot-hunter, Boer and Bushman, beast of the burrow and bird of the air, there was slaughter of springbok all around; and the time came when the only things left to see for miles and miles in the desert were millions upon millions of pairs of small, lyre-like horns.

The 'trekbokken' have vanished now, thanks to the barrel of the gun. But every so many years, say the old people, when the rains fall on that line at the correct time, there emerge from the sands millions and millions of daisies and each one, they say, represents a soul of a long-departed springbok.

Hopefully, all has not been lost. As a result of the conservation programmes funded by visionaries such as the Ruperts and Oppenheimers, and the establishment of the cross-border parks, there may yet come a time when our children's children will bear witness to such incredible spectacles, but this time without a gun in their hands.

Job Masego

J ob Masego was employed as a delivery worker in Springs in present day Gauteng when World War 2 broke out. He read about the war in the newspapers, but felt that it did not concern him until a visit one day by a close friend, Frans Makhanyua.

When Job opened the door that evening Frans stood there looking magnificent! He had joined the Native Military Corps and was in uniform. Job knew that the war was perceived by some as a white man's war. But he put aside the question of injustice at home and made the decision to fight for his country and freedom, like many thousands of black South Africans.

Job Masego joined the same unit as his friend and was posted to East Africa and then to Egypt with the 2nd South African Division. Here he was captured and placed in a prisoner of war camp. One day, sitting on the sand inside the barbed-wire camp in Tobruk, Job was thinking rather angrily about an event that had taken place the previous night. He had asked the Italian guards for washing water and they had arrogantly laughed in his face, remarking that he was already black and that washing would make no difference. When Job reacted indignantly, they had held him down and beaten him severely.

He was still furious as he absent-mindedly ran his hand through the desert sand. He felt something hard and smooth. It was a cartridge. It was not much use without a rifle, he thought to himself. As the area had not been cleared of debris before the camp was set up and having not much else to do, Job decided to continue to sift through the sand. He collected some 40 cartridges in all. Then it suddenly struck him that with the cordite contained in the cartridges, he could make a bomb and blow up something. Job systematically sifted and searched through the battle debris in the sand. He found pieces of fuse, which he was able to join into a four-metre length. He poured the cordite he had collected into a discarded milk tin. All of this he stuffed into his rucksack underneath his jersey and decided to bide his time.

Sometime later the prisoners were sent to the docks to carry cases ashore and it was there that the idea of blowing up a ship was born. Job's chance came on the third morning when, together with a number of prisoners, he was taken to a single-funnelled ship anchored in the bay.

Throughout the morning they were engaged in offloading supplies, mostly consisting of food. Having completed the job, the men were told that after lunch they would load cases of ammunition and drums and jerry cans containing petrol. Job knew this was his opportunity. He confided his plan to Koos Williams. 'This is our chance to get back at the Italians and also strike a blow for our people,' he said. 'But I will need everyone's help! When I am ready to place the bomb I want you and all the others to go over and distract the guards so that they'll not notice what I'm doing.'

The sun was setting as the end of the shift came and with it the opportunity to act. The men went over to the guards and Job slipped into the hold. He heaped straw over the milk can and soaked it in petrol. Leading a fuse, he scrambled up the ladder. He bent close to the hatch and touched the fuse with a lit cigarette. Luckily, his movements had not been spotted as the men had 'accidentally' dropped a case of ammunition overboard. The action had diverted the attention of the guards and only resulted in the culprit getting hit on the ear with the butt of a rifle. The ruse had worked. The prisoners were taken back to camp.

They sat in Job's tent waiting. Nothing was heard. Had the fuse gone out? Job went outside. 'Come!' he called to his comrades. 'Black smoke is coming from the ship!' At that very moment a sheet of flame appeared, followed by a massive explosion and then two more in quick succession. The guards appeared and hurriedly pushed the men inside.

39

The following morning the prisoners were marched down to the dock to carry on their work. The ship had all but disappeared and a number of drums were floating around in the sea. German officers lined up the prisoners and interrogated them in turn. Had anyone been smoking on board? Had they spotted any 'red balls' or mines in the water? The officers were forced to depart, none the wiser. The enemy was blissfully ignorant of the cleverly conceived plot!

Several nights later Lance-Corporal Masego and Private Masiya crept under the wire fence of their camp and escaped from Tobruk. They walked across the desert for 23 days sustained by a few meagre scraps of food saved from their daily rations. Just south of El Alamein, the South African Armoured Car Division picked them up and it was here on 16 November 1942 that Job's story was related to intelligence officers.

When the Eighth Army reoccupied Tobruk, navy divers were able to confirm the incident. Lance-Corporal Job Masego was awarded the Military Medal and the citation read as follows:

For meritorious and courageous action in that on or about July 21st 1942, whilst a prisoner of war, he sank a fully laden steamer – an F boat – while moored in Tobruk harbour. This he did by placing a small tin filled with gunpowder in amongst drums of petrol in the hold, leading a fuse from there to the hatch, lighting the fuse and closing the hatch. In carrying out this deliberately planned action Job Masego displayed ingenuity, determination, and complete disregard of personal safety, of punishment by the enemy or from the ensuing explosion, which destroyed the vessel.

Job Masego is a true South African hero and one whose brave deeds should never be forgotten.

The Rajah of the Eastern Cape

I n my ongoing search for interesting characters in our country's history, I came across an article that was first published in the *Cape Argus* quite some time ago and which was subsequently recounted by the well-known author, Frank Metrowich.

It is the story of one of the Eastern Cape's most colourful characters, General John Nixon. Nixon was born in England in 1825. He ran away to sea to seek fame and fortune at the tender age of fifteen and obtained a position as a cabin boy on a windjammer.

The ship's crew were a particularly brutal bunch even for those times and so badly did they treat him, that when the windjammer put in at Algoa Bay to replenish and obtain fresh water, young John decided to desert ship.

Slipping ashore, he immediately left for the interior. With no money, barefoot, and his clothes in tatters, he made his way. Eventually a kindly Boer family in the Uitenhage district, noticing his desperate plight, offered him sanctuary in return for his services.

For about a year John worked hard for the family, living the fresh outdoor life of a farm labourer. The climate did much to restore his spirits and health. Then, unfortunatly, the wanderlust returned anew and he decided to continue his interrupted journey to the East. Bidding a fond farewell to the family, he solemnly swore that he would keep in contact and having achieved fame and fortune, he would return to live amongst them.

He did write the occasional letter, but after a period of time the correspondence ceased. Nearly 30 years passed and people assumed that the young John had drawn his sword against fortune and lost.

Then, one day, an amazing thing happened. A ship, homeward bound from India, put into Algoa Bay and off it stepped a very distinguished military figure, accompanied by a retinue of bowing Indian servants. General John Nixon had returned to fulfil the promise he had made as a lad.

Amid much excitement he drove in state to Uitenhage to call upon the family for whom he had worked so many years previously. He decided to buy a nearby farm called Rietheuvel, which he very soon renamed Balmoral.

Here he set about building what was to become known as The Castle, a huge house with an elaborate castellated tower, crenelated battlements and lancet windows. The structure was modelled on Queen Victoria's residence in Scotland, Balmoral Castle.

He constructed a banqueting hall measuring 800 square feet, with a floor of specially selected yellowwood planks, brought up all the way from Knysna. It was furnished with beautiful rugs from the East. Sumptuous Indian silks adorned the walls and exquisite furniture was in abundance.

John Nixon was nicknamed 'The Rajah' as he entertained his friends and neighbours with great Oriental hospitality and in handsome splendour. It happened often that the house proved too small for the large numbers of guests and then tents and wagons were installed in the grounds. Many beautiful ladies were attracted to the banquets at The Castle and his parties would extend into the wee hours. He lavished priceless Oriental gems and rare curiosities on his favoured guests. Clad in flowing Eastern robes and sporting a turban, he would preside benignly over weekend parties that sometimes lasted as long as two weeks!

He did cut a dashing figure. His regal appearance, proud military carriage, awe-inspiring beard, bushy eyebrows and his long curly eyelashes made him irresistible to the ladies.

There was an occasional ruckus at Balmoral when the Rajah, during one of his drunken orgies, ran amok. He would seize a kukri, scimitar or similar weapon from the wall and, with bloodcurdling yells, set upon his faithful servants, in a determined effort to cut at least one of them to ribbons. The servants would flee for their lives into the surrounding bush. However, they soon learnt to keep a wary eye open and such occurrences, fortunately, never once ended in disaster. The servants remained in the bush until his anger subsided and life in The Castle would return to normal.

For some years the Rajah carried on this most extravagant life style and then, suddenly, he vanished, almost as dramatically as he had re-appeared. The story goes that he had sacrificed everything he possessed to save the life of someone he loved very dearly.

What really happened to cause John Nixon's fall from fortune, we do not know, though of his resultant decline in fortunes, we have further details. John Nixon, destitute and unhappy, returned again to India to try to recoup his losses. There he married and had a son named John. The son in turn became a general of great fame during World War 1. Fortune, however, refused again to shed its favour on the gallant Rajah and he died some time later, broken-hearted and in abject poverty.

John Nixon's beautiful farm was purchased some time later by the celebrated author and statesman, Sir Percy Fitzpatrick. In 1913 Sir Percy had visited the Sundays River Valley and was much taken with the land settlement schemes of the Addo Lands Company and the Cleveland Syndicate, which brought out British settlers and placed them on irrigated lands in the Sundays River Valley. Sir Percy thus decided to buy Balmoral farm located in the area. Soon the Sundays Valley developed into the major centre of South African citrus production and Fitzpatrick devoted most of his time to this cause.

Yet, it should be noted for posterity that it was in fact the Rajah, the celebrated General John Nixon, who had been the first to grow oranges in the Eastern Cape. Years before, he had called upon the assistance of Dr Brehm, a well-known Uitenhage botanist.

Dr Brehm, having heard about a new and marvellous orange

developed in Bahia in Brazil, had written away for bud wood. At about the same time a Mr Saunders from California imported buds from the same source. The South African buds, unfortunately, were taken from the wrong side of the graft. The American ones, by contrast, had come from the sport branch and soon citrus trees were flourishing in nurseries throughout Washington. The plants grown there were the origin of the Navel Washington oranges which are now famous the world over.

The Navel Washington, acclaimed as the king of all oranges, but for some quirk of fate, might quite easily have begun to flourish on a certain farm in the Eastern Cape and become known as the Nixon or Balmoral Navel!

James Chapman – A South African pioneer

J ames Chapman, a famous hunter and an explorer of the interior of South Africa, recorded his trials and tribulations in the now classic Africana book, *Travels into the interior of South Africa 1849 to 1864*.

James was born in Cape Town in December 1831. His father, James senior, came out to the Cape in 1828 and married Elizabeth Greeff, descended from a Flemish immigrant of 1683. In this regard it never ceases to amaze me how the Cape from its very inception became a melting pot as people from all over the globe migrated to the southern tip of Africa.

James Chapman senior was a bookkeeper, school and music teacher and an amateur botanist. James junior was therefore mainly educated at home, but he left the comfort of the family home at a very young age and travelled to Durban where he worked for a merchant. Later he was offered a senior clerical position in the Native Affairs Department in Pietermaritzburg. Yet again he became impatient with the sedentary life and, having learnt a great deal about the interior from colleagues, James decided to move on. He managed to get financial backing from a friend and two months short of his eighteenth birthday, he trekked up to the Transvaal in ox wagons loaded with merchandise.

James opened a trading store at Potchefstroom where he exchanged manufactured goods for cattle and ivory, carrying on a most profitable trade. He hired out men to hunt and trade for him, deep into the interior, and obtained goods on credit from a large number of firms in Natal. During a hunting expedition in the Schoonspruit area, near present day Klerksdorp, he shot his first lion and also met the famous artist and explorer Thomas Baines who, along with Joseph McCabe, was attempting to reach Lake Ngami in northern Botswana.

Chapman then trekked into Natal where he disposed of his bartered products and replenished his stock of goods. He returned to Potchefstroom in October 1850, with six wagonloads of goods, including 30 barrels of gunpowder. And this for a man yet to celebrate his 21st birthday!

His trading success in Potchefstroom incurred the wrath of Commandant H.S. Schoeman, a rival storekeeper, and we glean from Chapman's accounts that Schoeman used all manner of insults and threats, even assaulting Chapman's servants, and generally doing his utmost to drive the young Chapman from town.

It should be remembered that the Transvaalers were suspicious of any English-speaking person as a result of British actions against the Voortrekkers and the English seizure of the Republic of Natalia. The bitter trek over the Drakensberg following that seizure is commemorated by a statue of a barefoot trekker mother with her hand resting on the arm of a young child. The inscription reads: 'Liewe kaalvoet terug oor die berge, as onder die Britte ly'. Or, in English: 'Rather barefoot over the mountains, than to suffer under the yolk of British rule'. Go and see it sometime. It is located off the road to the Sterkfontein Dam in the foothills of the Drakensberg.

The young Chapman therefore came in for his share of contempt and bad treatment, although he recounted that there were many Afrikaaners that he liked and socialised with. It was probably the handicap of being an English trader and resident in Potchefstroom that contributed to his decision to leave and become an elephant hunter. In the winter of 1852, together with a certain Viljoen from the Madikwe district, he penetrated the unknown country north of the Magalagadi as far as the pan called Metsibotluko or Bitter Waters.

At the town of Matebe in the western Transvaal, Chapman was told by the missionary Inglis that Oswald and Livingstone had reached the Kilolo tribe at the Chobe River some twelve months previously. The news lit a flame of desire in the young man and he secretly planned to travel far north. As this brave, ambitious and sometimes reckless adventurer leaves the Transvaal on his first real hunting and trading expedition, let's pause for a moment and take in some of the facts surrounding a trek of this nature.

At that time there were no roads, only tracks, knowledge of which could be obtained only from local sources. So you had to send out riders in front of the trek to establish the best and easiest routes to follow the following day. Sometimes you followed the ancient elephant trails as that animal, being the biggest walking animal on dry land, has an uncanny ability to choose the easiest route through any terrain.

With your 'voorloopers' and 'agterloopers' and a full span of oxen, five laden wagons stretched across a kilometre. If you doubled the number of wagons, your trek would stretch across a length of more than two kilometres, which was a very difficult situation to handle, especially in hostile terrain. The oxen, sixteen per span, needed water at least twice a day and on a good day's trek you could cover ten to fifteen kilometres, compared to a good day on horseback when you could manage 30 to 40 kilometres. This is why, incidentally, so many towns in our country are located a day's horseride apart.

You carried everything with you, every single thing you required – except meat for the pot – from rifles, gunpowder, shot, spare lead, bullet-making equipment to foodstuffs – flour, maize, sugar, tea and coffee, dried fruit – and medicine. In addition, of course, there were the half-empty wagons taken along for the transport of elephant tusks to trade back at home.

When James Chapman left the Potchefstroom district he trekked up towards Lake Ngami in the north-western district of present day Botswana. A most striking feature of his descriptions is the enormous number of lions he encountered virtually on a daily basis. Most nights, sentries and armed guards were posted all around the cattle kraals. Men with flares stood next to the horses to stop them from bolting. Huge bonfires were lit and maintained throughout the night as the lions roared incessantly just beyond the peripheral light of the fires.

Of course, game in the area was plentiful at that time. Giraffe, hartebeest, zebra, kudu and a host of different antelope roamed the savannah. Also abundant were larger game birds like the gompouw or kori bustard and the 'wild turkey' or ground hornbill.

As they progressed the route became more difficult and the surroundings harsher. The group also discovered that the local tribes had a very deep-seated fear and even loathing of white people. Such attitudes were probably caused by the practices of slave traders, who captured men and women and frog-marched them away under the barrel of the gun, or the result of trekboer actions in which children were captured and taken away from the parents to be kept as indentured labourers. Such happenings certainly did not endear trekkers and foreigners to the local people.

Chapman recounts riding up to a Masarwa Bushman, who stood riveted to the spot, shaking from head to toe. On enquiring through an interpreter as to what the matter was, Chapman was told that the man wished to emphasise that the woman and two children accompanying him were his only family members. He was convinced, you see, that his family was about to be taken for him. Sympathetic to his plight Chapman went off to shoot an impala and gave it to the distressed man. Those were extremely hard and cruel times. Indeed, many acts took place that would not be tolerated by society today.

One of the more amusing encounters Chapman documented concerned a family of trekboers. These farming people hated anything remotely linked to things English. Chapman's expedition had a good few Bibles given to them by Inglis at Matebe. They presented one of the Bibles to the old Boer. His wife, however, able to read, noticed that it had been printed and published in London. She angrily hit it out of her husband's hand, saying that it was the work of the Antichrist. Then with two sticks she managed to lift the Bible up without touching it! She deposited it onto the fire. After burning the book, she dug a hole in the sand and buried the ashes. That was how deep Boer distrust of the English was.

I will not go into detail about the elephant hunting that took place in Chapman's time. Suffice is to state that it was like wholesale slaughter. Day after day, week after week! All in the name of accumulating that commodity known as ivory. If you have ever had the opportunity to view those old drawings, depicting thousands upon thousands of tusks laid out in the markets before being transported down to the coast for shipment to foreign shores, you will understand what I mean.

Let's leave James Chapman's adventures by recounting a last incident from his epic journey and one that made a deep impression on him. One day a Bushman came into Chapman's camp in an extreme state of agitation. He explained that a lioness had arrived at his home during the night, had parted the reeds of his flimsy hut and carried his wife away into the night. The man begged Chapman to accompany him to hunt down the lioness. They went to the little encampment, picked up the spoor of the lioness and tracked down the animal. On being aroused in a thicket of bushes, the lioness promptly picked up the body and started off. Chapman took aim and fired and the lioness went down.

What fascinated James Chapman most about the incident was the Bushman's explanation for his concern. He did not see killing the lioness as an act of revenge. Instead, he believed that it was only by killing the animal that his wife's spirit could be set free. If the lioness went free the spirit of the woman would be trapped forever.

Chapman's account is one of several, early travel accounts of the South African interior. Such descriptions provide important insights into our country's richly diverse natural and cultural heritage.

The Tyume
Valley

I f you ever have the opportunity to drive around the old Ciskei area, with its magnificent Katberg, Windvogelsberg and Amatola Mountains, I recommend you pull over to the side of the road in the vicinity of Keiskammahoek and Hogsback. Spare a thought for the people, black and white, who fell here, in a time now long gone. For, as you stand in the magnificent forest and mountains, you can sometimes sense that history and its terrible drama.

In this lovely Tyume Valley, lie the ruins of three old frontier towns established by Sir Harry Smith, whose ego led him to believe that he and he, alone, knew what was best for the Xhosa! The ruins in questions were once the beautiful little hamlets of Woburn, Auckland and Juanasberg. Sir Harry Smith had named Juanasberg after his Spanish wife whom as a young girl of just fourteen he had so gallantly rescued from being raped and murdered during the British pillage of Badajoz in Spain. Harry Smith, who was only 24 years old at the time, married her within two weeks. From that time onwards she faithfully followed her 'Enrique' to every posting and stayed near every battle he was involved in.

Land was granted in the area to soldiers who in return had to serve in the army whenever trouble erupted on the border. This all sounds very respectable but was not so after you learn that the land originally belonged to the Xhosa which was used as grazing for their extensive herds. It represented, in fact, the most fertile ground in the area. You will understand therefore why trouble flared and flared, again and again.

Yet, the white settlers in the area initially did not suspect any trouble. Many of the Xhosa seemed friendly and willing to work on the farms and so no provision for defensive operations was made. Then one day Soga, one of Sandile's councillors, paid a visit to Captain Stevenson at Juanasberg and warned him that the Xhosa were preparing to attack. He begged Stevenson to remove all the settlers before it was too late. But, in keeping with the superior attitude of many of those British officers, Stevenson took no notice of the warning.

It was dawn on Christmas Day 1850 when three soldiers of the Cape Corps rode out from Fort Hare to warn the settlers that war had begun and to order them to either group together as a defence or to fall back to Alice. The warning reached Juanasberg in time, but it was too late for the other villages.

At about 09h00 on Christmas morning, J. Shaw of Woburn was sitting on his veranda peaceful smoking his pipe. Suddenly, the sound of a shot rang through the valley and he fell dead from his chair. This was the attack signal and shouting warriors soon encircled the village. It was lucky that there were no women or children in the village. Only sixteen men under Lieutenant Stacey were present, together with Captain Stevenson from Juanasberg.

They ran to the half-completed church building, which proved of little use. The warriors surrounded them and opened fire. Lieutenant Stacey was the first to fall. The attackers started torching the village but the men held on bravely. Gradually, however, the ammunition began to run out and one by one the men fell. By noon on Christmas Day, it was all over.

Captain Stevenson had in the meanwhile managed to escape on his horse and was riding hard for Juanasberg to warn the people there, but he was stopped by a Xhosa man, named Festini, who informed him that a large body of Xhosa lay up ahead. Stevenson changed direction and fled to the Chumie Mission, the oldest mission station among the Xhosa. Meanwhile the Xhosa had split into two groups, half going to Juanasberg and the other half to Auckland. Despite Captain Stevenson's detour, all but three of the people of Juanasberg managed to reach the safety of Alice. The village itself was ransacked and torched.

Perhaps the saddest fate was reserved for Auckland, the most prosperous of the three villages. Its population consisted of 22 men and 30 women and children, none of whom had an inkling of events. Xhayimpi, a well-known induna, arrived with a large number of tribesmen. This did not cause alarm, as the villagers knew him well. The men mingled with the inhabitants and then suddenly at 14h00 that afternoon, Xhayimpi leapt to his feet, threw off his kaross and gave the signal.

The killing had begun. Nine of the Auckland men fell in the initial attack, while the rest ran for their rifles and headed to the half-completed building. However, during a pause in the fighting, the chief offered safe conduct for the women and children. At first they refused. 'We will die with our men,' they declared. But the men of the village persuaded them to leave. They sadly said their goodbyes and were led away by a young Xhosa woman, past rank upon rank of Xhosa warrior. All of them reached the safety of Gwali Mission Station, some twelve kilometres away.

Throughout that day and during the night the men in Auckland desperately hung on, hoping for reinforcements. But help never arrived. The end came on the following afternoon when the last of the three pretty little hamlets was ransacked and torched. I am not commenting here on who was right or who was wrong. I wish merely to tell the story, in order that we, as a nation, do not forget the many incidents that have made our history such an entangled and complex one.

Wattle trees in South Africa

Now that we are more eco-conscious, we should not forget the role that some of the exotic trees and plants have played in the formation of our country's industries and towns. The wattle tree, which is now an unwanted exotic, is a case in point.

The story starts as far back as the reign of William III, who set about improving industry in England. He recruited several Dutch families who were experts in various fields. The Van der Plank's, experts in wool and the manufacture of cloth, were amongst them. They settled in Smithfield and started a clothing factory.

John van der Plank was one of the grandsons of the immigrants. He loved sailing and the sea and, after calling on a certain Colonel Swanston recently returned from Tasmania, he decided to join the Colonel on a journey to Tasmania. At this time he met a Miss Louise White-Church. They fell in love but decided to marry only after his return from Australia.

On arrival in Tasmania, the ship's crew encountered a sandbar at the mouth of the Tamar River. John van der Plank offered to remove the sandbar. He was so certain of his abilities that he signed a contract. He promptly and permanently removed the obstruction. The Governor was greatly impressed and he offered John permanent employment. Delighted, John set sail for England to fetch his wife to be. Alas, back home, a quarrel ensued and Louise abandoned him to marry a doctor. It was then that John decided to buy a schooner and off he sailed to the Baltic to trade in timber.

After a number of ventures in and around the Baltic, he called in at Port Natal. He went inland to what we now call the Midlands, where he met many hardy Boer farmers and fell in love with the country. He had at last found the place he wished to call home. But, before giving up seafaring for good, he decided to make one more trip to Australia. His stay there was not long, but it became a very significant one for South Africa. One day, standing alone in the Australian bush, surrounded by wattle trees, he thought of the treeless country he was returning to. He took out a matchbox and gathered some wattle seeds.

John van der Plank later returned to his beloved Natal and planted wattle on his farm. It grew like wildfire. Farmers on trek asked him for seeds, which he gladly gave – until one day, when George Sutton from Howick became interested in the film of moisture, which lay between the bole and the bark. George sent it to London where it was identified as containing tannic acid. The leather tanners were very interested.

John van der Plank died in 1882, unaware of the mixed blessings he had bequeathed South Africa. Four years after his death the first exports of Natal wattle bark were sent to England. There were 39 packages. By 1898, 22 000 acres in Natal were under wattle and in 1900 a trial shipment of 500 tons was sent off to Australia. Wattle, it was found, could be grown and harvested cheaper in South Africa than in its native Australia.

In 1910 a forestry expert, Mr T. Sim, reporting on his observations in the Mount Edgecombe Estate, stated that after the tree had reached one foot in height, its average growth was one foot per month throughout the season. The wattle also proved successful in all soils, from pure sand to stiff clay and even in hard, dry soil.

At its peak, wattle covered over 700 000 acres in South Africa and the exports of wattle extracts and wattle bark during the 1950s was valued in excess of £6 million. There were eight wattle factories in Pietermaritzburg alone and the number of jobs created as a result was enormous.

The mining industry also grew to depend on the wattle, using stout wattle poles by the thousands. And it was the Australian wattle that solved a problem that had plagued the colonists at the Cape for some 200 years, that of drifting sands which made the journey from Cape Town to the interior very irksome. The wattle or Port Jackson succeeded where everything else had failed, in stabilising the long stretches of sand dunes on the Cape Flats.

This tree which did so much for employment and economic improvement in our country, stands today as a damned exotic, but its present status should not prevent us from acknowledging the role it played in our economic history.

The land and its issues

With the land invasion issue in Zimbabwe causing headlines in the international press and some unsuccessful attempts at land occupations in our own country, it might be appropriate to have a look at the situation from a new perspective. What light can the history of times gone by, shed on this?

Clearly, the land issue is an extremely contentious issue. During the time of the old Zuid-Afrikaansche Republiek (or Transvaal Republic), a law was promulgated which entitled every male who had reached voting age to two farms of not less than 6 000 morgen each. These farms were distributed to the burgers by the State. The question arises of course as to how the State itself acquired the land to re-distribute so freely.

The barrel of the gun, in most cases, is the answer. Let me hasten to add that this did not occur only in the Transvaal, but over the entire country. Dutch expansion into the hinterland took place by displacing the Khoi-San people. British expansion took place in the Eastern Cape by forcing the Xhosa from their ancestral lands. The Xhosa in fact fought a series of nine frontier wars in defence of their independence, which cost the British over £4,5 million – a tidy sum especially in nineteenth century terms. And still these wars did not break the might of the various tribes in the Eastern Cape. Instructions were given to Sir George Grey to pull back the 1820 Settler farmers and others and to resettle them inside the old boundaries of the Cape in order to return the land to the Xhosa. Then came the Nongqawuse cattle killing and the might of the Xhosa was destroyed.

What is disturbing to learn is that Thesiger, later Lord Chelmsford, immediately after the end of these wars, led the British army from the Eastern Cape up to Zululand and commenced the destruction of the Zulu kingdom. I am not a politician but an historian who likes to relate historical events in broad, brush strokes. This makes it difficult for me to ignore the fact that stories of land dispossession are seldom told and until fairly recently, history has in general been recorded by the Victorious and not by the Vanquished.

The Cape Colony

In 1828, the missionary Dr John Philip made this statement about the indigenous people of the Cape Colony. 'In the century and a half of Dutch rule here, the Hottentots have been despoiled of their lands, robbed of and cajoled out of their flocks and herds ... and with few exceptions [they] have been reduced to personal servitude, under circumstances that rendered them more helpless than the slaves with whom they now associate.'

The disintegration of Khoekhoe society was a relatively swift process as leadership in that society was very dependent on the possession of stock. With the continuing loss of grazing lands and no means to recover these, the larger groups went into a downward spiral leading to total impoverishment.

The Dutch, in the course of colonising places like Banda in the East Indies, destroyed indigenous societies, exiling survivors in order to make way for plantation agriculture. In parts of the Moluccas they systematically smashed peasant communties. And, although it was not done in this direct way at the Cape, we have to face the fact that the destruction of indigenous communities was mainly the result of actions by Europeans and not some faceless Imperial God.

It was indeed the process of land-grabbing by farmers that tore apart Khoekhoe and San society and allowed white settlers to establish farms across the whole colony, south of the Orange and west of the Gamtoos River. Later, the settlers met up with the agricultural Xhosa who, as mentioned earlier, eventually also lost their lands in what has been termed 'The Hundred Years War'. The European conquest of the Cape Colony and other areas of what was later to become South Africa, proved to be a very violent process.

Guerrilla-style wars came to typify the resistance of the herders and hunters or the Khoi-San. From the Griqua attacks on the northern border in 1701 to the last Kora attack at the Orange River in 1879, some one 178 years later, the same trend was revealed. As European farmers penetrated deeper and deeper into the interior of the Cape, they brought about the steady and successive impoverishment of each region. They lifted stock and expropriated grazing and waterholes. Life for the indigenous people as anything other than as labourers for the white farmers, was made totally impossible. Resistance was inevitably the result.

Once we begin to understand these processes, the Khoi-San wars against the invading farmers become intelligible. The attacks on farmers were often by herders who had lost their own sheep and cattle. The so-called Bushman raids against the expansionist farmers were nothing less than the resistance of the hunter-gatherers in defence of their hunting grounds, their veldkos and their very means of an independent livelihood.

The north-eastern Orange Free State

It has long been said that the land distribution between black and white South Africans was an historical accident and that after the movements of people set in motion by the Difaqane, vast tracks of land were left uninhabited and open for the taking. This is probably only twenty percent accurate. The reality of the coercion and dispossession of Blacks of their lands is far more complex and far less flattering to the White pioneers.

Prior to the Difaqane, the north-eastern Orange Free State area was one of the heartlands of the Sotho peoples. It was the home of the Tlokwa Chiefdom and today eight generations of Tlokwa chiefs lie buried at Nkoe near Verkykerskop, just north of Harrismith.

In 1821 after that area had been devastated by Hlubi refugees from the wars caused by the rise of Zulu power in the Natal Lowlands, the Tlokwa under the legendary Queen Manthatatisi moved south and west, raiding, pillaging, and dispersing other groups and tribes. Eventually, under her son, Sekonyela, the Tlokwa settled in the Caledon River valley where Moshoeshoe decisively routed them and Sekonyela was forced to flee south of the Orange River. Sekonyela's brother, Mota, moved back to the original Tlokwa homelands and settled near the newly-created village of Harrismith where a sizeable community took root. But already by 1850 a great deal of the land in the area had become alienated by Whites who had established claims on the basis of their own laws.

The law at the time stipulated that a condition for land ownership was a six-month residency, but in reality even this was evaded. Thus most of the land fell into the hands of aliens, with much speculative capital coming from Natal and from town dwellers generally. The Norse family, for instance, held large tracks of land in and around Memel. British officers, like Henry Green and H.D. Warden, became big property-owners during the period of British sovereignty up to 1854. Storekeepers and traders like Adolph Coqui owned some eleven farms in the area.

A land surveyor, K.J. Kock, recounted that a land commission in 1860 had undertaken an inspection of 250 farms in 32 days and that each farm was no smaller than 6 000 acres.

As more and more White farmers settled in the area and as the Tlokwa community continued to grow, the settlers began to agitate against the Tlokwa. They sought to secure their permanent removal. The State had in fact decided that the Tlokwa would be moved, when in 1850 the war against Moshoeshoe intervened. The Tlokwa agreed to assist the Boers against Moshoeshoe in return for the promise of land. In 1861 it was decided to establish Mota's followers on land on the Mill River, leased by Commandant Cornelius de Villiers from D.C. Uys.

To understand what then transpired, it is important to identify each of the role-players. There was the Tlokwa tribe, now under Chief Letika Tsotetei, and the Kholokwe tribe, led by Chief Hlomise, who had been expelled from the Witzieshoek area. The farm on which the tribes were settled was leased to De Villiers, who managed to convince fellow Volksraad members to pay him a portion of the hut tax collected from these tribes, as well as to exonerate him from his lease payment for the land. The Volksraad voted him £60 per year retrospectively to 1861. De Villiers then bought three farms in 1867 for £1 560. It was at this point that he began to show a talent for fraudulent land deals.

In 1868 De Villiers warned the tribes that he was expecting an influx of White settlers in the area and urged them to buy two farms from him. They secured the title in return for 4 000 head of cattle. But the truth of the matter was that De Villiers was involved in gross fraud as the land – all 2 190 square miles of it – had already been granted to a number of White settlers, living as far away as Durban, Bloemfontein and Cape Town. De Villiers unashamedly continued to buy farms in the area and to sell them to Blacks.

When eventually his deeds were discovered, he was stripped of his rank and salary. The Volksraad then offered the farms for sale to the two tribes who, of course, now bereft of their cattle, had no means of payment. And so, at Mill River, as elsewhere in the Harrismith district, legitimate owners ultimately lost their right to the land.

From 1870 onwards the tribes became increasingly alarmed at the number of new White settlers in the area. Eventually, when some Whites arrived to occupy land, which the Tlokwa and the Kholokwe said belonged to them, a skirmish broke out and two tribesmen were shot dead. If one compares this incident to numerous similar incidents that took place at the Cape in an earlier period, the pattern remains the same. Such apparently small incidents seem to herald the beginning of the end. Two White men, Botha and De Jager, were acquitted of murder, but the incident made a very deep impact on both white and black communities in the region.

The 1870s also witnessed a growing discontent against the Sotho by the White farmers, who sought to extend their control over Sotho lands and labour. The resultant scarcity of land within what was allowed as Black settlement areas finally undermined the independence of the tribes.

It is sad that the political struggles of such people find little place in the published historical records of today. Unfortunately, it is not only segregationists, but historians, anthropologists and even Africans themselves who have chosen to delete from memory those groups who failed to find a triumphant place in history.

Griqualand East

The Griqua under Adam Kok II lived in the Philippolis area. Encroached on by the settlers and constantly harassed by the British under the likes of Sir Harry Smith, the Griqua decided to move from the area. In desperation, they asked the British to tell them where they could go to be rid of that country's rule forever. The British recommended that they relocate to the no man's land north of the Transkei and south of Zululand, in present day Griqualand East.

Their trek over the Maluti Mountains, blasting their way through the roughest mountains in this country, rather overshadows the efforts of Retief and his party in their trek through the Kerkenberg Pass in the Drakensberg. Down the mountains, through the present day Matatiele, the Griquas went, to eventually establish the little village that to this day bears their leader's name, Kokstad. Relatively well armed and supplied with horses, the Griquas succeeded in establishing a loose hegemony over what is today the Mount Currie, Umzimkulu and Matatiele areas.

Under Governor Sir George Grey, the Cape lent support to the Griquas, a situation that continued for a while. Other tribes in the area like the Bhaca came under Griqua control. Farms of 1500 morgen (just over 3 000 acres) were parcelled out, but this resurgence in Griqua fortunes was short-lived.

Boundary disputes with expansionist colonial Britain broke out and after 1874 Britain took more direct control of the area. The continuing disputes led to the community's loss of land and created widespread anxiety. This growing tension, like a festering sore, reached a climax in 1878 when the Griqua rose in revolt in defence of their independence. Yet, history has shown how often such a scenario actually suited the

British. It gave them a reason to put down the revolt and at the same time to properly colonise the area. And that's exactly what happened.

During the 1850s traders had come down from Natal and settled in the Umzimkulu area. The Strachan brothers, Thomas and Donald, as well as George Brisley and Edward Stafford set up partnerships and became wholesale traders in the area. Donald Stafford became the first magistrate in the district and even gave military assistance to the Griqua when the Bhaca took exception to Griqua rule. But this all had happened in the early period. As the disputes unfolded, it was these very same pioneers who ended up holding vast tracts of land.

Such is the background to Griqua dispossession. Once a landed community closely allied to the British colonial administration, they had within a relatively short space of time become a collection of landless people, harbouring a very deep-felt grievance. In the years 1896–98 under the leadership of Andries le Fleur, this Griqua disaffection turned to militancy. Some individuals ended up in court and eventually prison. Tragically, the Griqua as a whole were forced to disperse and eke out an alternative existence by relying on their skills as transport-riders, artisans, woodcutters and herders.

Some twenty years later, the old prophet Le Fleur returned and tried unsuccessfully to regroup the Griqua. He led them on a trek to the Karoo, but as this area had become inhabited and cut up into sheep farmlands, the move only succeeded in dispersing the tribe further.

That is how the Griqua people of mixed European and indigenous ancestry, who had owned and occupied land from Blinkwater (Griquatown today) in the west to Kokstad in the east, became a landless people, scattered far and wide across the country of their birth.

The Pedi and Mafolofolo

Professor Peter Delius has produced two wonderful books: *The land belongs to us,* dealing with the history of the Pedi people in the nineteenth century, and *A lion amongst the cattle,* concerning the politics of Sekhukhuneland. They give us extremely valuable insights into peoples, places and a time that all South Africans should be aware of. It is as a direct result of historical events such as are sketched in Delius's books that our differing approaches and opinions have been shaped over time.

As we drive towards the scenic Mpumalanga lowveld, with its majestic beauty and numerous game reserves, many of us do not realise that we are travelling through an absolute treasure trove of history. In the eighteenth century the Pedi had become a powerful people and by 1800 Paramount Chief Thulare – with his capital in the beautiful Steelpoort River Valley – was raiding as far south as the Vaal or Lekoa River, westwards to the Magaliesberg and northwards as far as the Soutpansberg. In those days there was a thriving trade in ivory, horns, skins and metal goods. People living in the area of the north-eastern Transvaal occupied a strategic position, linking the traders from Inhambane and Delagoa Bay with the people deep in the interior.

In the nineteenth century, the Pedi vied for control of the land against the powerful Swazi kingdom to the east and this tension was exacerbated in 1845 by the arrival of a group of trekkers who immediately laid claim to the land and started subjugating their neighbours. Local young people had to leave for the Cape to find employment to be able to buy guns and keep the threat at bay. By 1860 an uneasy stalemate existed between Paramount Chief Sekhukhune and the trekker community at Lydenburg.

At a place called Botshabelo, 'The place of Refuge', a band of Pedi Christian converts under Rev. Alexander Merensky built a mission station. This group had left the territories of Paramount Chief Sekhukhune in 1864 with their leader, Johannes Dinkwanyane. By late 1870 Botshabelo boasted 1 600 inhabitants, a mill, a store, a wagon-building shop and the largest school in the Transvaal at that time. At the heart of this settlement was the church, built by the converts from stone, bricks and thatch. Interestingly, Botshabelo remained a thriving educational and religious centre until, at the height of apartheid during the 1960s, it was declared a black spot and all its tenants and peoples were removed and their homes destroyed. Today a few of the old structures still stand, including the church, the mission and Fort Merensky.

Despite the provision of educational facilities and the industrious nature of the community at Botshabelo, there were mounting internal conflicts at the mission. The elders questioned the missionaries' intolerance of age-old practices and beliefs like initiation, lobola (bride wealth payment), rainmaking and the fertility festival. Many were also angered by Merensky's refusal to allow them to acquire land in their own right and they were rightly embittered by the missionaries' insistence that they meet and respect Boer demands for payment of tax and supply of labour.

These grievances led to the decision in 1873 by Dinkwanyane and 300 of his followers to leave the mission, but they were faced with a difficult choice. If they stayed in the Transvaal the Boers would not have allowed them to acquire land. If they returned to the Pedi they would have had to abandon the Christian faith. Instead they chose to settle in an area that was located on the margins of both Boer and Pedi control and, alongside the Spekboom River, they built Mafolofolo, or 'The Place of Gladness'.

They surrounded the entire village with a high, stone wall pierced by shooting holes. Inside lay further fortifications, caves and a necessary supply of water. At the heart of the settlement, they again built a church large enough to accommodate the entire community on Sundays, which during the week doubled up as a school.

Dinkwanyane was trying with great difficulty to create a Christian land-holding community independent of direct control by the Pedi and the trekkers, but in the Transvaal of the 1870s there was no room for Mafolofolo. Local farmers and officials saw the community as a profound threat to their authority and demanded its destruction. Local missionaries, fearing that it would become a magnet for their converts, refused to provide religious assistance for the village and some even agitated for its destruction.

It was the absolute determination to bring Dinkwanyane to heel that caused the outbreak of war in 1876 between the Pedi and the Zuid-Afrikaansche Republiek. During the battle the Boers, who had linked up with the Swazis, marched on Mafolofolo. Having failed to breach the outer wall with their four-pound canon, the Boer forces hung back and let the Swazis do the fighting. After a desperate battle, the Swazis managed to breach the town's defences, and Dinkwanyane and most of his followers were killed.

It is a pity that the story of Dinkwanyane and his community at Mafolofolo is so little known. Against immense odds they had tried to blend a Christian value structure with their African culture. They were responsive to a changing world and the solutions that they adopted speak very powerfully to present day South African realities.

I am further convinced that everybody in our beautiful country should be made aware of the past, including the various histories of the land. This knowledge will help to create a better understanding of the major issues that we have to deal with today as we consider what is right and what is just.

Maria Espach

'**D**o you want to kill yourself? You must be mad to think that you can go out in the rain with this fever upon you!' With difficulty the young woman forced the sweating man back upon the sodden blanket. The rain dripping through the tent had turned the floor into mud that oozed up between her toes. She was barefoot. She never wore shoes these days. It was just easier that way.

The bearded old miner protested. His concern was that if he did not work his claim for a period of three consecutive days, the law said officials could 'jump' it. She reassured him: 'I will go down to the Mining Commissioner. He must understand that with an epidemic of malaria and typhoid here in Pilgrim's Rest, you will all die if you don't recuperate properly.' Maria Espach gave her patient a dose of quinine, hitched up her skirt and walked down the hill to the shack of Angus MacDonald, the resident mining commissioner.

Hundreds of little tents lined the river. People had arrived because of the news of a gold discovery. On 5 February 1871 Mr A.F. Jansen, landdrost of Lydenburg, had informed the Executive Council in Pretoria of a find of alluvial gold by Messrs Parson, MacLachlan and Valentine, at a spot six hours ride east of Lydenburg. The first real gold rush of the Transvaal had begun and within thirteen weeks the President of the Zuid-Afrikaansche Republiek had proclaimed the diggings open to the public.

The many hundreds of prospectors and diggers slept alongside the claims they had pegged. There was little or no sanitation. Food and provisions came at a premium. Once the monthly fee of five shillings had been paid to the Commissioner, the only thought the people there had, from sunrise to sunset, was to dig for gold. Malaria and typhoid began to take their toll, quickly reaching epidemic proportions.

It should be remembered that during those days there were no qualified nurses in South Africa. The sick and the dying were left to care for themselves as best they could, using quinine, of which there was little enough. The only commodities available in quantity were gin and whiskey, but at a price, brought from Delagoa Bay on the heads of handpicked, good-looking young women who were then sold as 'house maidens' to the rough and tough miners.

The landdrost at Lydenburg was at his wit's end. Very soon the miners would be spending more time digging graves than digging for gold. The outbreak of disease threatened to spread to Lydenburg.

Listening one day to such expressions of concern was Maria Espach, an orphaned niece of a local man. She suddenly burst out, 'I have decided that I want to go up there and nurse the sick miners.' Her stepfather was aghast. 'You are out of your mind to suggest such a thing. That is no place for a woman. A rough drunken lot they are, and you will run the risk of falling ill yourself,' he told her.

Maria, being a tough-minded girl, was not to be dissuaded. The following morning she visited every store and household in Lydenburg and collected as much equipment and quinine as she could beg, borrow or steal. She persuaded her uncle to drive her in his cart to Pilgrim's Rest.

The incessant summer rains had set in and the area was infested with malaria-carrying mosquito. Her first problem was to persuade the men that their health was more important than the gold they were digging.

As she stumbled down the hill in the rain to the shack of the mining commissioner, Angus MacDonald, she realised that if she was to secure the health of the diggers, the law had to be changed. She put her case to MacDonald. 'I see your point,' he replied, 'but I have to be strict about this. Every day I get people wanting to peg claims and it isn't fair on the hard-working workers to allow a man to peg a claim and for him not to work it.'

Maria replied: 'As things stand now, men are dying. They force themselves to dig in fear of loss. This must change!'

MacDonald was impressed. 'You are a very determined and brave lady, and there are many men here that owe you their lives. I will do as you ask,' he promised.

Some time later when the President of the South African Republic went to the diggings on an official visit, he was astounded at the number of Scots there and called the area Mac Mac. Introduced to Maria, he asked if she was also Scottish. 'No,' came the humble reply. 'I'm an Afrikaans meisie, but married to Mr Austin. My maiden name is Espach.'

The following day a group of miners visited the house where the President was resting and asked to see him. They were rebuffed but remained insistent. The President heard the noise and came out to enquire what the disturbance was. 'We have come to ask you to do something for us,' they said. 'We want the State to strike a medal to honour all the wonderful work Maria has done. For this purpose we have collected the gold from the grateful miners.'

Exactly a year later Maria Austin was presented with a gold medal in the form of a Maltese cross, together with a handwritten letter from the President. It read:

My dear Madam

I hand over to you the accompanying Burgers Cross as a token of sincere respect and acknowledgment, on behalf of myself and the public of the Goldfields, for your kind and devoted services rendered to those in distress.

I feel sure that I express the feelings of all when I say, 'May God reward you for your noble self-denial'.

Trusting you may be spared many years to enjoy the fruits of a noble work nobly performed.

I remain, my dear Madam
Your obedient servant
Thomas Burgers
President, South African Republic

The Burgers Cross is a unique award in our country's history. It was the first one ever issued by a President in South Africa. It was also the first official award made to a woman in South Africa and the first to the nursing profession. For the rest of her life until she died at over 70 years of age, Maria continued to devote her life to nursing. Her achievements have become the stuff of legends.

The Lost City of the Kalahari

Across the mists of time comes the story of an ancient city built by an unknown people in an era long past. An interesting thing to consider is that Mapungubwe ('the hill of the jackal'), in the Limpopo province of South Africa, may also have been a mythological place had it not been rediscovered in 1934 and removed from the realm of myth for all of us to see today. Today, at last, Mapungubwe's world-famous gold bowl, sceptre and rhinoceros are on display at the University of Pretoria.

The legend of the Lost City of the Kalahari may have its beginnings in antiquity, but we pick up the threads in the early 1880s. At that time G.A. Farini, an American showman, while conversing with a Bushman during a roadshow, learnt of the legend of the Lost City. Farini and his son, Lulu, decided to find this mysterious place. They trekked up through the northern Cape and into the vast dry Kalahari Desert. They took local guides from a place called Mier who told them of an ancient ruin and people with sacks made from animal bladders, full of diamonds.

Having completed the epic journey and made his way to London, Farini claimed to have found the ruins of a city in the desert. He installed an exhibition at Westminster Aquarium including in it artefacts, sketches, photographs and even maps of the city and its location. He intimated that the architectural style of the city was similar to that of ancient Egypt and Phoenicia and on 8 March 1886, he delivered a paper to the prestigious Royal Geographical Society in London.

The world was stunned and the story has, indeed, continued to intrigue people ever since. Dr J.N. Halderman, a chiropractor from Pretoria, was so taken by the circumstantial evidence that in June 1958 he made his first expedition into the desert to search for the ruins in the sand. Some thirteen expeditions have subsequently been undertaken to try to find that legendary place.

There had been relatively little drifting of sand between Farini's journey in 1883 and when Halderman set out in 1958. Halderman's hopes were, therefore, very high. He covered 8 400 miles by air and over 2 000 miles by car. But in the area where Farini claimed to have seen the city, he found only a very large sand dune.

Undaunted, in 1959, Halderman undertook a second expedition to the area. On this occasion Marthinus Drodsky, who had discovered the famous Drodsky Caves in Botswana, accompanied him. In 1950 Drodsky had met two Bushmen who had told him of these famous ruins and he had made a journey with them. However, after two weeks of effort and when it seemed that they were very near the area, the men suddenly warned Drodsky not to proceed. They feared that local Bushmen were going to ambush and kill them all. So agitated had they become that Drodsky was forced to turn back.

Drodsky, incidentally, was a remarkable man. No one understood the Bushmen and the Kalahari as he did. It is said that in his youth he could run a steenbok down over fifteen kilometres and kill it by hand. He could live off the desert just like the Bushmen. He had learnt Bushmen hunting techniques and their arts. He knew, for instance, how to crawl down a porcupine hole with a two-metre, sharpened stick. Then, when close to the porcupine, to scrape a mound of sand in the tunnel and lunge with the stick through the sand to kill the animal without being covered in porcupine quills.

Drodsky was himself convinced of the truth of the Lost City story. He was as keen as Halderman to solve the riddle in a second attempt. But, alas, this expedition also came to nothing as, indeed, have all other subsequent expeditions!

Who knows what may still be lying under the ever-moving Kalahari sands? It is possible that as a result of recent inventions and new technologies we may be on the brink of the rediscovery of the Lost City of the Kalahari. No one should stop us from dreaming!

In memory of
a legend

In the dusty old cemetery of Ventersdorp lie the earthly remains of one, George Frederick Shaw, an Irish-born soldier who had joined the British forces and was posted out to the western Transvaal during the Anglo-Boer war. Soon after arrival in South Africa, Shaw met and fell in love with a young Afrikaans girl by the name of Martha Engelbrecht.

At about this time Lord Roberts had captured Pretoria. He had realised that the Boers were not going to surrender and he had passed that most fateful proclamation to burn down Boer homesteads and detain women and children in concentration camps.

As fate would have it Shaw was given the job of destroying Martha's homestead. On arrival the troops gave the three womenfolk the customary ten minutes to pack their personal belongings before torching the farmstead. Martha ran out onto the lawn and sank on her knees in front of her lover. Tears streaming down her young face, she pleaded, 'How can you possibly burn my home? You are my lover. We have had such good times here and this home is filled with such precious memories, how can you possibly do this deed?' Well, he couldn't. He turned his back on the homestead and marched his men back to camp, leaving the homestead untouched.

The commanding officer was furious and, in the argument that ensued, he thundered, 'If that's the way you feel about the Boers, Shaw, why don't you go and join them.' And Shaw did just that. That night he stole from the camp, buried his uniform, and joined the Boer forces, obtaining a job as an unarmed transport rider and given the responsibility for caring for the three women while the men were on commando. We all know the outcome of that war. The British won and the beautiful Schoonspruit Valley was burnt to the ground, all the way from Klerksdorp to Ventersdorp.

Shaw was captured along with many other Boers. The British troops did not recognise him as he was wearing civilian clothing and had grown a beard. One morning the prisoners were being handed rations when the sergeant shouted, 'Attention!' Of course the Boers did not react but Shaw, being a trained soldier, snapped to attention. The game was up.

They arrested and court-martialled him for desertion, found him guilty, gave him a pick and a shovel and marched him off to the cemetery to dig his own grave. Shaw was tied to a chair that to this day is still with the Leask family, who are descendants of the family in Klerksdorp. He was blindfolded and then shot to death by a firing squad. Unbeknown to everyone, Martha who was now pregnant was hiding in a thicket of trees at the side of the cemetery. She was forced to bear silent witness to the killing of the man whom she so desperately loved. Perhaps as a form of consolation or to provide a father for her baby, Martha soon afterwards married Shaw's best friend, John Fleisher. John gave the baby boy his name.

After the sad events of Shaw's death a fresh posy of wild flowers was found on his grave and, when the townsfolk enquired, the cemetery attendant told them that a woman had placed the flowers there in the early hours of the morning. Every week of every month of every year, for over 40 years, fresh flowers were lovingly placed on Shaw's grave.

When Martha died, the local dominee remarked during the sermon, 'Many waters cannot quench love, neither can the floods ever drown it, for love is as strong as death, and jealousy as cruel as the grave.' The full significance of these words was not understood until recently when a fellow historian, Rob Milne, and I began to research the story.

We tracked down John Fleisher junior. He was living on a farm outside Ventersdorp where he was being looked after by Tannie Susie

Deneker. He was 101 years old at the time. We interviewed him for British Channel 4 television. Eventually the story came out, though he was loath to discuss it as he believed that his mother had been wrong to place flowers on Shaw's grave, especially after John Fleisher had given her such a good life.

The old man agreed to draw us a map of where the old homestead was and where Fleisher and his mother had brought him up. Rob Milne and I then located the mainly wattle and daub dwelling and on the same grounds the dwelling in which John grew up. We took photographs of the area and only when they were developed did we realise what the dominee had been referring to at the graveside. You see, behind the house were the remains of an apple orchard, and alongside the house on the left-hand side was planted a single pine tree and on the right-hand side a pepper tree. Exactly the same trees flanked Shaw's grave in the old cemetery.

And so we read in the Song of Songs in the Bible:

> In the apple orchard I awoke you;
> Take no love to yourself but mine;
> Set me as a seal upon thy heart;
> For love is as strong as death;
> And the coals thereof are the coals of fire
> Which has a most vehement flame;
> Many waters cannot quench love
> Neither can the floods ever drown it.

John Fleisher junior passed away recently at the age of 103 and, with his passing, the only remaining, living link with this now legendary South African Love Story has disappeared. Go well John!

Japie Greyling:
a brave Boer lad

On 31 May 1902 the peace treaty of Vereeniging was signed, bringing to an end the terrible war that racked our country from 1899 to 1902. One hundred years have passed since then and the passage of time has healed many of the scars and dissolved much of the hatred that is the characteristic result of all wars. Yet, it is important that we remember and learn from these events; and the story I'm about to tell is one well worth remembering.

James Seeley, a captain in Queen Victoria's imperial army, was in a foul mood. He had spent weeks in the saddle going from farm to farm, trying in vain to trap the ever-elusive Boer commandos. It was no fun traipsing about in the Orange Free State sun and meeting with such hostility from the Boer women and children. The hatred was so great you could almost taste it and the Boers under the command of General De Wet were nowhere to be found.

A scout arrived with information and was escorted into the tent by a young lieutenant. Jacobs was the man's name and he was one of the best and most reliable spies in the pay of the British forces.

'Well, man, what have you to say for yourself?' the Captain demanded.

Jacobs replied: 'Yesterday morning I was passing the farm of Meneer Greyling, which lies 30 miles east of here, and I saw some horses in the kraal and a number of men sitting around at the side of the house drinking coffee. Meneer Greyling and his wife and another man – a big man with a full reddish beard – were sitting on the stoep. I was sure they were part of a commando, so I went up and asked for some breakfast. They gave me mealie meal, biltong and coffee; and the bearded man started questioning me. I told him that I was on my way to work for my cousin who had a farm about twenty miles away near the Transvaal border. He said I would be lucky if I found it still there, as the English had been burning the farms and taking the women and children off to concentration camps. He then asked me if I had seen any British soldiers.'

'What did you say?' asked the Captain.

'I lied, Captain, and told them that there were soldiers some 60 miles in the opposite direction from your camp,' said Jacobs.

The Captain was delighted. 'Well done, Jacobs,' he said, 'go and get yourself something to eat, for we'll be leaving for the farm within the hour and you are to lead us there. Lieutenant,' he commanded, 'pick twenty men and supply them with rations for four days. We will ride through the night and get there just before dawn.'

It was not an easy ride. The ground was rough and the going hard in the dark, particularly for the horses. At dawn they spotted the sleeping farmstead.

Captain Seeley rattled off instructions: 'Lieutenant, take ten men and skirt around the back. I will give you fifteen minutes and then I'll come in from the front. Shoot anybody who tries to escape.' After fifteen minutes Seely gave his patrol the order to advance at a fast canter. They had reached some 400 yards in front of the house, when the Boers suddenly took flight. They galloped around the spur of the koppie, disappeared around another corner and then vanished altogether. After searching in vain, the pursuers gave up and returned to the farmhouse.

Young Japie Greyling, only eleven years of age, was leaning against the doorpost when a British officer, accompanied by ten men, dismounted in the yard. The officer pushed the boy aside and with a revolver in his hand entered the house, followed by five men ready to shoot at the first sign of trouble. But all that the search uncovered was Japie's mother and his two sisters.

One of the men who could speak a little Afrikaans asked the young boy who he was. 'I'm the son of my Pa and you will never catch him,' the reply came.

'Where did the Boers go?' the officer asked.

'To their command,' he replied.

'Where is the commando?' Captain Seeley snapped.

Japie retorted, 'I will not tell you.'

'Oh yes, you will,' the Captain said, grabbing him by the shoulders and shaking him. 'If you don't tell me where the commando has gone and the name of the commandant who was here, I will have you shot, right here in your house.'

Japie looked at him straight in the eyes and said slowly, 'I will not tell you, I will not betray my father.'

'Lieutenant, take the boy to the wagon house over there and pick six of your best for a firing squad,' commanded the Captain. The young officer hesitated. He wasn't squeamish, but he was being asked to shoot a mere boy in cold blood.

'What are you waiting for?' demanded Seeley between his teeth. The lieutenant turned to his men. He called out the names of six men and marched them, along with Japie Greyling, to the wagonhouse, followed by his commanding officer. 'Put him up against that wall!' the command came. The lad was as pale as death and for a moment it seemed he was about to burst into tears.

'This is your last chance,' said the Captain. 'Tell me now, or you will be dead in two minutes. Where is the commando and who was the commandant?'

With his fists clenched tightly against his thighs, Japie declared, 'I won't tell!'

'Get ready to do your duty lieutenant.' The young officer went pale as the lad stood there resolutely, his back to the wall. 'Prepare to fire,' the lieutenant commanded. The soldiers each went down on a knee, loaded their rifles, and took aim.

Just at that moment the old woman servant ran into the house screaming, 'Ounooi, come quickly, they're shooting klein baas Japie dead!'

Seeley walked swiftly over to the lieutenant and said softly to him so that the boy could not hear, 'You're not to fire. You'll give no order.' The Captain then strode up to the slender figure, standing ramrod straight, his mouth slightly open and a curious expression of expectancy in his eyes. The Captain said urgently to the boy, 'Come on, tell me quickly. You have only a few seconds left. Where is the commando?'

In a voice scarcely above a whisper came the reply, 'I will not tell you.'

The English officer smiled and grasping the boy's hand said quietly, 'I hope I shall meet you again someday – you are surely the bravest young man I have ever known. At ease men!' the command came to the firing squad. Rifles were lowered and the men stood up.

At that very moment Japie's mother came running out of the house, her arms held out imploringly and shouting, 'Oh no! Oh no! Don't kill him!'

In a moment, Japie was in her arms.

Thirty years later, recalling this incident in his memoirs, General Seeley wrote: 'As long as I live I shall never forget that wonderful moment when love of father, home and country triumphed over certain death. Never shall I forget the expression on the face of that Boer lad when he looked up, his eyes brimming with tears, and said to me, "I shall not tell."'

Some six years later General Seeley, then Lord Mottistone, returned to South Africa and tried to find the young man, who had defied him with such supreme courage. But alas, for all his searching he was unable to locate the man whose brave deeds had made such an indelible impression on him.

The demise of the Bushmen or San

It was not long after Van Riebeeck landed at the Cape in 1652 that he heard tales of a people called the Sonqua, but several years passed before the first recorded contact was made. We are told of a Dutch official named Wintervogel who came upon a party of Bushmen on the Berg River; and this place of encounter is still known as Sonqua's Drift.

The Bushman or San lived in the interior and were described by the settlers as 'an entirely wild nation, without cattle or houses, but well armed with hunting bows and spears'. The Europeans did not initially perceive them as a serious threat, although at this time three Dutch burghers, engaged in shooting hippo in the Berg River, were murdered by Bushmen. Such remained the status quo for nearly a hundred years.

According to their mythology, the Bushmen had originally come from the north. They entered the area of the Great Karoo, where they found vast herds of game. Let me add that this migration took place thousands of years before the arrival of the Dutch. George William Stow, a pioneer in Bushman research, spent many years patiently copying rock paintings and gathering artefacts and stone implements which, as he stated, were 'unquestionably the title deeds of the Bushmen'.

The caves of the Bushmen and their ancestors are richly adorned with painted scenes of trance dancing and their intimate relationships to nature. It was here too that they roasted their 'uintjies' or bulbs, pummelled their grass seeds and stored dried locusts for the coming

80

winter. They also roasted termites, still today called 'Bushmen rice'. And with the arrival of the full moon they danced the 'mo-koma', or dance of blood, in which both men and women would leap about, around and around in a circle, until the trance state was reached, and the blood gushed from their nostrils.

The Bushman did not cultivate plants but their knowledge of bulbs, herbs, trees and scrub was intimate and deep. It represented the accumulation of centuries of information passed down from the beginnings of time.

The secrets and stories of these people are absolutely fascinating and should you be interested in finding out more, I would recommend that you read books such as *Miscast* by Pippa Skotnes and *Stories that float from afar* by Professor Lewis-Williams. The astronomical knowledge of the Bushmen never ceases to amaze me. After Dr W.H. Bleek had mastered the Bushman language and written down the legends, 'The dawn's heart' and 'The dawn's heart child', it became apparent that the Bushmen had been observing with the naked eye movements of the planet Jupiter, and its satellites, long, long before European astronomers.

Incidentally, lions never bothered the Bushmen. If lions were encountered during the day, the Bushmen would run directly at the animal, shouting at the top of their voices and waving their arms. Seeing such unnatural behaviour, the lions would simply turn tail and flee! At night they sprinkled on the fire a special ground powder made from a fungus, which grows only on anthills. Lions found the smell so repugnant that they kept a wary distance.

The Bushmen watched, year after year, as the white man entered their traditional hunting grounds. At first they did not protest. In the course of centuries the pace of settlement picked up. The farmers trekked to the land where the present town of Ceres is to be found and named the area the Warm Bokkeveld because of its vast herds of springbok. Then they entered the area higher up and named it the Koue Bokkeveld.

From the Bokkeveld, the settlers went to the Roggeveld, where wild rye used to grow and before the 1750s they had settled in the Calvinia

81

district, which the Khoekhoe knew as Hantam. Ten years later the valleys between the Langeberg and the Swartberg had been settled and the more adventurous farmers had begun entering the Nuweveld area around present Beaufort West. In time the area of the Camdeboo (meaning 'Green Heights' in the Khoekhoe language), lying between the towns of Graaff-Reinet and Aberdeen, was occupied. On the west, the settlers made their way up into Namaqualand, as far as the Kamiesberg and by 1760 there were white farmers in the Sneeuberg range.

Year after year, decade after decade and century after century, the Bushmen watched in growing horror the unstoppable creep of European farmers over more and more of their land, a process which forced them to withdraw progressively further from their home grounds.

A fundamental difference between the Bushmen and the Europeans was that the Bushmen hunted primarily for food and then only on a small scale, while the settlers hunted to eat, but also to sell meat, skins and ivory. They even hunted 'for fun'. When a Bushman hunted, he did so with a simple bow and arrow that had a limited range, so the game usually had a fair chance. The hunt was long and difficult. The white man hunted with a musket! This was like murder in comparison.

However, the stage was set, the cauldron of conflict was starting to boil and during the 1770s it boiled over. A farmer named Coetzee van Reenen sent a white overseer to look after his flocks along the banks of the Zak River. It was known that he was a brutal man who shot Bushmen people for no reason. There were many farmers like the overseer who considered the Bushmen not to be human beings. The Bushmen eventually retaliated, and slew the overseer with an assegai.

It was revenge for all the horrors suffered under this man. On the farmers' side, however, it was considered murder with no extenuating circumstances. A strong commando was sent up to the frontier and many hundreds of Bushmen were massacred. As soon as the commando had departed, the Bushmen rose up as one. From the Kamiesberg in the west to the Stormberg in the east, they went on the rampage. Farms were ravaged and farmers and their families brutally murdered. As a result, more commandos were raised and the wholesale slaughter of the Bushmen began. It was the start of a guerrilla war.

Prisoners were sometimes taken all the way down to Cape Town. In 1772 a band of 58 men and women, of all ages, was tried for the murder of Roggeveld burgher Hendrick Teutman, his wife and daughter. The most gruesome punishments were handed down. All the children were flogged, the women were hanged and the men were killed by means of 'breaking' on the wheel.

Some years later when the famous botanist, Thunberg, was travelling in the Roggeveld, he came across a commando that had killed over 100 Bushmen. The commando told him of another detachment that had wiped out over 400 in the Sneeuberge alone. It became the policy of the Dutch East India Company to exterminate the Bushmen and in the nine-year period between 1786 and 1795 at least 2 500 were killed and more than 600 captured. Not many men were taken alive for they usually fought to the last arrow.

Shot, powder and handcuffs were readily supplied by the government for such expeditions. A surgeon's report on one particular conflict contains a significant statement concerning the attitude of the people. He stated quite simply: 'The Bushmen have no fear of death.'

The last stand of the Bushmen in the Sneeuberg area has been recorded and makes for poignant reading. The Bushmen had retreated into the mountains and were surrounded by a commando. Cut off among the rocks at the edge of a precipice, they fought for the last time. One after another, they fell as the sharpshooters fired, until only one man remained alive. As the man put his last arrow to the bow, the commando leader touched by the man's bravery, called out and told him that if he surrendered, his life would be spared. The Bushman looked at him and shouted, 'A chief knows how to die,' and, releasing his last arrow, he jumped off the precipice. For many years sun-bleached bones could be seen on the ledge far below.

During the nineteenth century Dr Bleek, his daughter and Lucy Lloyd befriended Bushman convicts working on Cape Town's breakwater. They learnt the Bushman language and worked hard at preserving some of their beliefs. In 1875 Dia! Kwain told the following story to Lucy Lloyd. It concerns a dream about the death of Dia! Kwain's father. She recounted his story as follows:

When I was with a Boer, I dreamed that we were cutting up a sheep. The Boer came to us as we were cutting it up and said that he would beat us to death. The dream spoke to me thus, and I told the Boer not to kill us...for I did not want him to kill my father... I would work out both what I owed and what my father owed. And the dream said to me that I saw my father lying dead in the Sun's heat. AND I WEPT.

And I asked the Boer, did he think it was such a big thing that we had killed, that he acted like this? I dreamed that the Boer drove us before him...

And when day broke, I arose and told my wife that a dream had told me that we were cutting up a Boer's sheep. I saw my father standing there dead. And the wind was in the north, and I asked her, did she not see that the sky looked like it was going to rain, just as the dream had told me, that the dust was covering the sky. Therefore I should go and talk to the Boer about the ox, I should see what was happening that had made me dream of father, that the Boer had killed us. The dream had told it to me, just as if a person had spoken. Therefore we will go home, we will go and listen at the huts, and see whether we do not hear news...

And my father's eye was blinking before I was gone.... Rainwater, which was not little, was falling. I said to my wife...you seem to think that my dream was not clear. I shall see things that my dream told me about. I SHALL SEE IT. THEN YOU WILL SEE.

We returned home to where we lived with the Boer and we stayed two nights...the wind blew, as if it was begging from me, just as the wind had done in my dream when I dreamed about father that...the Boer had killed us...when the sheep bleated. The dream had told me this.

And my mother said to me that I seemed to have disbelieved the dream and to have thought I should see father again, though the dream had told me I should not see him again. Yet, now I saw her, and she had come to tell us that father had died leaving us…and mother asked me, did I not see that the dream had spoken the truth…So the dream I had told her about had not deceived me…

The springbok had afterwards passed the hut, as if they were not afraid, mother did not know where the springbok came from. They were not few and they came and played as they approached the hut were my father lay dead. The springbok appeared to be moving away. And the wind really blew following them. THEY WERE RUNNING BEFORE THAT WIND.

It was really father's wind, and you yourself feel how it is blowing. You know it used to always blow like that whenever my father was shooting game.

I spoke to my wife and told her about it. I asked her whether she did not realise that I was feeling my inside that was biting.

As the wind blew past I felt my insides biting….

I felt that when one of my people was dying.

MY INSIDE ALWAYS ACHED WHEN IT WAS ONE OF MY PEOPLE.

This complex description is not the product of a savage mind but represents a poetic vision of a people with a unique understanding of family and nature. Today, tragically, only small groups of the Bushmen people survive and I can say with pride that I have had the privilege of spending time with them in the Magalagadi Desert in Botswana. It was an experience I shall never forget.

The rinderpest

From the vastness of Central Asia and the dawn of history, came the scourge of the rinderpest. The most dreaded plague of the pastoralist, even to this day its name sends shivers down the spines of farmers.

It was war that spread the rinderpest in Asia as the Roman Empire staggered into decline, with wave after wave of so-called Barbarian invasion. The Huns from Central Asia, the Alans from the Volga, the Austrogoths from southern Russia and the Visigoths from Hungary; each invading force brought in its trail, the rinderpest.

Charlemagne's conquests caused tragic cattle losses in the ninth century. The invading Mongols of the thirteenth century brought fresh outbreaks of the dreaded disease. The wars of Louis XIV witnessed an epidemic of rinderpest through Poland, Hungary, Prussia, Austria, Germany, Switzerland, Italy, France, Holland and England, leaving one and a half million cattle dead in the fields.

Then the onset of the Napoleonic Wars again brought an outbreak of rinderpest. However, it was only later that that killer disease arrived in Africa. This occurred in 1889 when the Italian army was doing battle in East Africa and, as usual, the disease marched with the army. At the end of that year, we find the rinderpest sweeping through Masai land. By 1892 it had reached Lake Nyasa and by the end of 1895, enormous numbers of cattle and game were dying on the banks of the Zambezi River. Then on 3 March 1896, the cattle sickness appeared in Bulawayo.

There were urgent calls to the Cape and elsewhere; and, finally, there arrived from Pretoria a young Swiss veterinarian, Arnold Theiler. After a diagnosis of the dead animals, an announcement of the grave situation was made. The rinderpest disease was on the march into southern Africa. It was moving at thirty kilometres a day – the pace of an ox. Angry warriors in Matabeleland blamed the coming of the white man for the disease. Within a couple of days, 244 white farmers were massacred. This rebellion, coming just after the Jameson Raid, almost ruined Cecil John Rhodes. It cost one million bags of grain to settle the discontent as, without their cattle, the Matabele would starve.

Rinderpest was known to be a malignant and highly contagious fever, one of the principal symptoms being an acute inflammation of the mucus surfaces with a temperature and a discharge from the eyes and nose. This was followed by a short illness and within a week the animal was dead. Infection usually took place through the mouth and resulted from contact with infected animals.

A conference was called in Mafeking and P.H. Faure, Minister of Agriculture in the Cape Colony, stated categorically, 'If you do not compensate for healthy cattle, there will be secrecy.' And how correct his forecast proved to be in the months to come. On 3 March the disease had reached Bulawayo; by 10 March, Palapye, on the road to Kimberley; and by 16 March, it was in the Tuli Block, near the Transvaal border.

At Palala, in Botswana, the authorities attempted to stop the spread of the disease by setting up a cordon. About 100 African transport riders were trapped north of the cordon. Their cattle appeared healthy, but they knew that with the passing of time, the disease would overtake them and they would lose their cattle. Had the authorities been prepared to pay compensation, things might have worked out differently. The authorities were unwilling to pay, however, and on 20 March the transport drivers, in desperation, stampeded their cattle through the line at Palala, fleeing southwards in the hope of saving their cattle. They carried the disease with them and sealed the fate of the entire Bechuanaland. By 31 March, the plague had advanced 750 kilometres south of Bulawayo and was 25 kilometres from the Cape border.

The slaughter of cattle now became enormous. In the Mafeking district, 87 950 died of a total of 90 000 cattle. At Vryburg only 6 300 of the 86 964 animals survived.

Almost as quickly as the disease spread, so household remedies sprung up to 'cure' the animals. One of the so-called remedies was a mixture of brandy and salt fed daily but, apart from producing a hangover, this had as little effect as indeed did another remedy of camphor mixed with milk. In Griqualand West a farmer marketed three different 'cures' using onions as a base. Even Joseph Chamberlain, British Secretary of State for the Colonies, went on record recommending some bizarre remedy. The results remained the same. The animals kept dying and fences proved useless in the spread of the disease. Within a couple of months over 10 000 head of cattle in the Orange Free State were lying dead in the fields. For a while it looked like the fence along the Orange River might hold but then that hope gave way.

The veterinarians had of course been busily trying to find a remedy. In February 1897 Doctor Koch finally announced that the disease could be prevented in healthy animals by immunisation. Injecting the animal would produce the mild effects of the disease, but it would then have a permanent immunity. However, this cure came very late and at an enormous cost. Of a total of 1 639 435 cattle in the Cape, no less than 575 000 had perished. Estimates in the Orange Free State were between 45 000 and 60 000 dead.

Today in South Africa rinderpest has become only a name but for many earlier generations of Africans it was a measure by which to recall the past. That was the Year of the Rinderpest, it used to be said.

The Karkloof glider

As the old road to the interior climbs out of Howick in KwaZulu-Natal it passes through a mountain range called the Karkloof. In about 1845, as the story goes, a Dutch farmer was travelling along the road in a heavily-laden Cape cart. As he crossed the valley his horses took fright, swerved and overturned the cart. Nobody was injured, but the wreck of this cart lay there for years. This is the origin of the name Karkloof and it is one of the most beautiful areas of the Natal Midlands.

Many people settled in this most pleasant place and among the most interesting was John Goodman Household, the son of a settler who had emigrated from Britain in 1850. In the early 1870s Household conceived of a plan to fly. Roaming around the surrounding hills, he watched eagles, vultures and other raptors gliding over the valleys and soaring on the updrafts. He decided to shoot a vulture and having carefully measured its wingspan and noting the weight to span ratio of the bird, he worked out the proportions of a glider that was big enough to carry his own weight. Working with stout bamboo, a few lightweight steel tubes, oiled silk and very thick paper, Household completed his first glider. It included a pilot's seat, like a swing, suspended from the wings on four ropes. But the glider would not fly.

Being a determined sort of chap he then set about constructing a 'Mark Two'. When this contrivance was completed, the pilot and his brother, Archer, assisted by a few Zulu men, trundled it one moonlit night to the top of a ravine. Of course all of this was done in complete secrecy, for fear of parental displeasure and public ridicule.

After much practice and great effort the glider was eventually launched from the cliff edge and away into the evening shadows soared the intrepid young Household. He skimmed the tops of the trees and climbed to almost 120 metres, crossing the valley that was almost a kilometre and a half in width and, finally, attempting to land on the far side.

Unfortunately, the controls of the glider were very crude. It slid, side-slipped, stalled and crashed into a treetop. Household was catapulted into a pool of water and broke his leg! The glider was wrecked and during the unfortunate pilot's confinement to bed, the heap of twisted metal and fabric was dumped in the loft. John's parents saw to it that he never repaired it, and as time passed the historic glider was thrown on a rubbish dump and forgotten.

Thus ended what was almost certainly the earliest attempt in South Africa to fly. What a pity the glider could not have been preserved and displayed for all to see!

Chief
Tshatsu

Throughout our troubled and often stormy history, South Africa has produced many men, black and white, who have achieved fame like Job Masego, Jan Smuts, and Nelson Mandela, and those who have gained a measure of notoriety like King Shaka and Scotty Smith. Here's a long-forgotten story of a man who was heir to the chieftainship of the Ntinde, a minor tribe of the Xhosa, and who captured the imagination of the British people. Unpretentious as he was, he became the most spoken about and sought-after black man of his time.

As a young boy, Jan Tshatsu was given for schooling to Dr Johannes Theodorus van der Kemp who lived at the Bethelsdorp Mission Station north-west of Port Elizabeth. Jan was one of the mission station's first pupils. He learnt reading, writing and carpentry and progressed on to a study of Christianity, which eventually led to his conversion. On occasions he would preach to the local communities of Khoekhoe people.

Jan Tshatsu later returned to the Ntinde to succeed his father as chief. In 1835 we find him with his small group of about 1 000 men, women and children living near Grahamstown on land granted to him by a dubious hero of yesteryear, Colonel Sir Harry Smith. Here the Rev. John Brownlee had opened a mission station and life was relatively peaceful, although Jan had incurred the enmity of the Xhosa for refusing to become involved in one of the frontier wars. As he sat sunning himself in front of his hut, he would never have imagined that within a very short time, he would be the idol of British society. Fate was about to play its hand.

Dr John Philip, that champion of the 'coloured races' in South Africa, was preparing to depart from Bethelsdorp for England to give evidence to the House of Commons's Aborigines Committee. He had made up his mind to take two people with him as proof of what had been achieved and what could be achieved in South Africa among the indigenous people of the Eastern Cape. After careful consideration, he chose a Gona (Khoekhoe) man from the Kat River Settlement, named Andries Stoffels, and Jan Tshatsu.

It should be remembered that these missionaries were then the bane of the colonial government's life and were also hated by the Eastern Cape settlers for their perceived interference and their insistence on justice for the indigenous peoples. It was to prove an important visit. The group set off on the journey to Cape Town to board a ship for England.

The British philanthropists greeted the testimony of Dr Philip with enormous enthusiasm, but the statements of both Jan and Andries excited even more interest. The two men eulogised the work of the missionaries and slated and condemned the colonists for starting the frontier wars. They gave accounts of people being beaten and murdered, with no recourse to justice. They told how they had been robbed of their lands and how Sir Harry Smith had commandeered the missionaries' house for his own residence and had turned Jan's home into stables for his horses.

When the group spoke at Exeter Hall, the headquarters of the philanthropic movement in Britain, they were given a standing ovation. They were taken on a tour of England and spoke at meetings up and down the country. They were fêted, wined and dined by royalty and aristocracy alike. The two men were a sensation and Dr Philip was hailed as a national hero.

Unfortunately, the trip to England did not conclude happily. Andries Stoffels never returned to the Kat River Settlement as he died of consumption in Cape Town. Jan Tshatsu did return to his Ntinde tribe, but when the next frontier war broke out, he cast off his European clothes and lifestyle and joined the Xhosa in an attack on Fort Peddie.

Jan Tshatsu's punishment was harsh. John Brownlee deprived him of his church membership and Sir George Grey confiscated his land on the banks of the Buffalo River. I sometimes wonder how you and I would react if we were forced to witness our farm and grazing lands, the lands of our forefathers, being slowly and systematically taken from us.

Fountain Ravine, Table Mountain – the story of an escape

There are numerous stories in our country of daring escapes, but this one has an element of luck so statistically improbable that it is worth recounting. In the late 1800s a Table Mountain Club member, Mr Searle, was climbing a particularly hairy part of the mountain called Fountain Ravine, some 800 metres above sea level. Here he came across a rather large cave and on entering he found it to contain the remnants of habitation. He noticed a soot deposit on the roof and came across a calabash, iron, as well as small animal bones in a midden. Later, he led a second expedition up to the cave and more articles were unearthed.

For many years, people could only speculate as to who had spent time in this desolate part of the mountain, although the artefacts did provide some idea of the era concerned. Some fifty years later, one of the Club members was studying a manuscript from the United States of America, published in the early 1800s, entitled *The life and adventures of Joshua Penny*. It turned out that Joshua Penny was an American citizen, who had been pressganged into the British navy and forced to serve on the HMS *Sceptre*. While his ship arrived in Table Bay, he had plotted his escape.

He began by reporting ill and the ship's doctor instructed two of the mates to carry Joshua to the hospital in town. No sooner were they opposite the first grog house than Penny declared that he was thirsty and offered to buy the drinks! Needless to say, he took that opportunity to escape. He purchased what he required and set off up Table Mountain.

The reason he chose the cave in question was related to its inaccessibility. Fires that were made inside could not be seen from the town and it was situated near a spring of water. In those days there was a lot of wild game on the mountain and, after hitting a small buck off the side of a precipice, he grilled the meat and kept the skin to fashion clothing and sandals. What Joshua Penny did not know was that the HMS *Sceptre* had been shipwrecked in a gale force wind and was no more.

Joshua initially had a hard time adapting to the lifestyle, but he very soon came to the conclusion that it was better to exist like a hermit than to face the English. For over a year he lived in this wild and free state, killing and eating buck and dassies and collecting wild vegetables and fruits, even managing to brew a potent alcohol. In later life he was to say that it was one of the nicest times of his entire life.

One day Penny noticed that the entire British fleet had sailed from the Bay and he decided that it was time for a change. He walked down the mountain and into town. He approached a certain Captain for a working passage. The Captain was so aghast at Penny's appearance that he asked what stood before him – animal, vegetable or mineral! Fortunately, Penny was able to secure a passage and, safely on board the *Brigg*, having shaved and dressed in a sailor's uniform, he quietly enquired as to the whereabouts of the *Sceptre*. 'You see that small object to the left of the Castle,' they explained. 'That's a monument to her officers and crew.'

Joshua Penny sailed away never to return to Cape Town, but when the publication that I referred to earlier, was discovered in the 1950s by the club member, material testimony to Penny's life resurfaced. At that point, the Mountain Club decided to go back up to the cave and after an investigation and some digging, Penny's knife, a tinderbox, as well as parts of the British naval uniform that were consistent with the period, were recovered. In this way the first firm evidence to link Joshua Penny to the mysterious inhabitant of the cave in Fountain Ravine was revealed.

HMS
Birkenhead

It was a proud Captain Robert Salmond who stood on the bridge of HMS *Birkenhead*, watching the young recruits boarding the first iron vessel in the service of Her Majesty's Royal Navy. Mere lads, they had looked splendid marching down from the barracks to the quayside, dressed in the scarlet and blue of England and the tartans of the Scottish regiments. Women and girls had lined the streets and cheered them on as a fife and drum band led the men. The swagger of the kilts and the cheering of the crowd certainly made it a day to remember. But then that's how it is when men go off to war – often great excitement followed by even greater sadness.

It was January 1852 and the *Birkenhead*, docked in Cork, was loading the new recruits, mostly Irish lads. They had joined the British forces as a way of escaping the devastating effects of the potato blight of the 1840s, which had resulted in thousands starving to death, leaving the economy of Ireland in tatters.

The men were destined for South Africa, to bolster the troops Sir Harry Smith had requested for purposes of fighting another frontier war against the Xhosa. Lieutenant-Colonel Alexander Seton was the Commanding Officer. Aboard there were: 25 women; 31 children; one naval surgeon; seventeen ship's officers; twelve military officers; three military surgeons; 125 crew and 479 soldiers and other ranks. This was a total of 693 personnel.

The cargo included 350 double-barrelled carbine rifles and gold bullion to the value of £250 000 for payment to the troops on active service in the Eastern Cape. The journey southwards was not a pleasant one. They hit enormous storms, the hatches were battened down and for a whole ten days rain lashed the ship as it tumbled and ploughed through the roughest seas imaginable. So bad was the trip that six women went into premature labour. Most of the women on board were accompanying their husbands or were intending to visit their loved ones in South Africa. They were housed in the stern.

Anne Chapman, whose husband Bill was one of the ranks, was going out to South Africa for the first time. While on leave her husband had returned to England to fetch her. She was pregnant with their first child and they intended to settle in the Eastern Cape.

On the night of 26 February, the *Birkenhead*, having left Simon's Town, was steaming along the coast in the calmest of waters. The night was perfect. She was just short of Danger Point, about two miles off the coast. 'Fifteen fathoms' came the voice from the night watch forrard, 'What's our course?' the night officer Davies enquired. 'S.S.E. by E. Sir,' came the reply from the helmsman. 'Twelve fathoms,' the watchman said. Davies frowned, 'We must be on shelving. Probably sand. Eight fathoms.' There was a tone of alarm in the lookout's voice. Mr Davies reached for the speaking tube but in vain. The submerged rocks ripped into the *Birkenhead*. The troops on the lower deck stood no chance. In the engine room the men were cut down by scalding steam and as the great paddles slowed down, the screams of the women and children aft could be heard. The *Birkenhead* had struck a reef and she was breaking up.

'Get all the women and children up on deck,' commanded Lieutenant-Colonel Seton. 'Davies, lower the starboard paddle boat.'

The mate looked at the Captain, his face ashen. 'The gig has staved in, Sir. They can't loosen the big boat amidships.' 'Then take all the women and children to the two little cutters, and load them immediately,' Captain Salmond instructed Lieutenant-Colonel Seton. 'I'll expect your men to stand on parade until the women and children are clear of the vessel.' With the blast of a bugle and the roll of a drum, the men were formed into their regiments.

Just then Anne Chapman came across to the Captain. 'Please, let me go to my man', she pleaded. 'No, he is on parade,' Seton replied. 'But you don't understand I am with child,' she begged. 'All the more reason for you to get into the boat,' the Captain gently encouraged. 'It would be the way your husband would have wanted it.' Anne Chapman was taken away and the two cutters soon lowered into the sea.

As the women and children pulled away, they heard singing, initially quite softly and then gathering in volume. It was the hymn, 'Abide by me'. The women sobbed and wailed and then slowly became quiet. Watching the men standing to attention on the deck of the stricken vessel, the women joined in the song. Together they sang their final farewell.

The ship lurched in a swell, broke apart and then sank. Some of the men managed to cling to bits of flotsam and debris in the water but very soon the sharks arrived and a feeding frenzy started. Later, the cutter *Lioness* arrived and picked up 116 survivors from the wreck. In total 445 lives were lost that night. Only 193 persons survived.

I am told that there are certain regiments that continue to hold a formal dinner on 26 February, where they sing 'Abide with me' as a tribute to the men of the *Birkenhead* who established and gave such perfect form to the heroic maritime practice, 'Women and Children first'.

There is a plaque at Danger Point commemorating the bravery of those courageous and steadfast men who did not rush the little boats, for fear of swamping them. I suggest you go and see it sometime.

Henry Hartley

enry Hartley arrived in South Africa from England at the age of eight with his 1820 Settler parents. In 1846 he moved away from the conflict on the Eastern frontier to a town called Andries-Ohrigstad, which was named after the Voortrekker leader, Andries Pretorius, and Ohrig, a German pioneer trader who had helped develop the little town. Here Henry was granted a trading licence, but as the town had many problems of its own, he moved on once again.

He joined forces with some of his 1820 Settler friends, including James Jennings, on New Thorndale, a farm on the southern slopes of the Magaliesberg. Hartley, Jennings and Frederick Selous became famous elephant hunters and stories about Henry Hartley are particularly numerous and recounted throughout southern Africa.

One of the most well-known of these relates to an event that took place while he was out elephant hunting with his sons. They had been stalking their prey most laboriously and were lying in hiding, waiting for a chance to shoot, when a lion rather inconveniently came prowling around. The sons wanted to shoot the beast, but old Hartley did not want to disturb the elephants after such a long and hard chase. He crept up on his hands and knees behind the bush where the lion was sitting. Suddenly, he lifted his head above the bush, shook his massive beard, and let off an almighty roar. The lion bolted for its life and the Hartleys, needless to say, shot the elephants.

The lives of those old elephant hunters in the Magaliesberg were not very romantic. They would kiss their wives goodbye and then trek into the wilderness. The road wound northwards past Holfontein and Klipfontein, and along the Madikwe River to a place named Wegdraai. Here the returning hunters bade farewell to the old river and turned to travel on to the Limpopo River.

They continued up to the Tati area on the border with Botswana and Zimbabwe where it was believed the ancient Ophir of the Bible had once been located. Then further on they went to the Zambezi Valley where they hunted elephants. It was there they came to a halt and began the return journey. Home for only a brief period, they kissed their wives goodbye once more and trekked down to the coast with their ivory. Eventually they returned to the farms, but only to start the process once again.

Some time later, Henry Hartley met the famous explorer and cartographer, Karl Mauch, and together they set off to the Tati area to see the ancient gold workings. On 28 November 1867, Hartley and Mauch returned from their upcountry visit. Mauch had been prospecting and was convinced that he had discovered an enormous gold field. He told his story to the *Transvaal Argus*, whereupon the entire world sat up and took notice.

All over Europe, America and Australia, the newspapers printed the story, billing it as the rediscovery of King Solomon's Mines. Wild rumours abounded. People spoke in grand and glowing terms of the thousands of ounces of gold taken by the Ancients and the countless thousands of ounces still waiting to be taken. The first gold rush had begun. Many sorts of people, from every corner of our planet, packed their bags for South Africa and, having arrived, enquired about the road to the north.

Sir John Swinburne, another famous character, arrived in Potchefstroom with Thomas Baines, the artist and explorer. The town was booming. Almost every shop stocked the supplies necessary for prospectors on their long trek northwards to the Tati Concession area. Sir John Swinburne headed for Tati and Baines for the New Thorndale farm to meet Hartley. Hartley agreed to accompany Baines on a journey to the goldfields and Baines's subsequent sketches and paintings made on the expedition have become extremely rare and prohibitively expensive. Most are now housed in institutions in South Africa and Britain.

Not too surprisingly, Hartley's hunting adventures eventually led to his death. Some time after the trip with Baines, he went out hunting. He shot a rhino, watched it fall and then walked up to the animal. But it suddenly stood up, tossed him into the air and then fell down dead, literally on top of Hartley, breaking several of his ribs and injuring him internally. Although Hartley continued to hunt after the accident, he died a few years later, on 8 February 1876, aged 61.

If you ever get the chance to drive out of Gauteng and through the lovely little hamlet of Magaliesburg, take the Rustenburg road and, as you cross the railway line for the second time, Henry Hartley's original residence can be seen on your left. It has been renovated and converted into the most delightful bed and breakfast in appropriate Victorian style. Further down, as you turn off to the right and wind up the hill to Chippy Brand's wonderful Mount Grace Hotel, you will find a little pub called Hartley's. The pictures adorning the walls relate to some of the stories I have mentioned. Henry Hartley's life will never be forgotten. So memorable a figure was he that Rider Haggard used him as the basis for the character of Alan Quartermain in the very famous novel, *King Solomon's Mines*.

And, if you know where to look on the western side of the Magaliesberg station, you will find the ruins of the old Magaliesberg Hotel where Haggard and his mates would regularly meet. What interesting tales such walls hold safe!

How Adderley Street was named

On many occasions over the last couple of years I have been asked how Adderley Street in Cape Town was given its name. And so, here is the story.

Let's go back to the 1840s when we find Sir Harry Smith holding office as governor of the Cape Colony. His popularity had waned somewhat. The Boers had friends and family in the Cape. Many of the colonists felt that the British annexation of the Orange River Sovereignity leading to the Battle of Boomplaats had been unnecessary. The policy of no pay and no compensation for Eastern Cape farmers called to arms to serve in the numerous frontier wars and forced to leave their loved ones vulnerable on the farms, was also proving unacceptable. These and other matters contributed to a growing political movement for self-government at the Cape, led in large part by prominent settlers of British origin.

In this social climate came the rumblings from the Colonial Secretary, Earl Grey, of another piece of bad news. A despatch arrived in 1848 stating that the Cape was to be included amongst those places to which British ticket-of-leave convicts or prisoners on parole would be sent.

In a private letter to Sir Harry Smith, Earl Grey stated that the British government was faced with the problem of ridding Britain of Irish political offenders and that it was not possible to send them to Bermuda, New South Wales or Van Diemen's Land. Grey here conveniently ignored the fact that the social structure at the Cape was more complicated and potentially more explosive when compared with that of New South Wales, Van Diemen's Land or Bermuda.

Sir Harry Smith in turn did not foresee that sending political convicts to the colony would prove to be problematic, although he was certainly against the idea of the Cape becoming a permanent penal settlement for ordinary felons. He was under the impression that the Cape Legislative Council would not be opposed to having these 'misguided' people as settlers in the Colony. Sir Harry Smith could not have been more wrong! The Council was furious. Heated debate ensued. Smith realising that he was not going to get his way shouted angrily at the members: 'Be careful, or some of us may subject ourselves to the same pains and penalties which these gentlemen of Ireland have incurred, and a passage for us be found to some other country.' 'It was the duty of the Cape,' he went on, 'to help the mother country, as she had helped the Cape in the past.'

The legislature was up in arms. It was not going to be bullied on this occasion and Mr J.B. Ebden in particular was very vociferous. Local newspapers like the *South African Commercial Advertiser* carried angry editorials.

In November and December 1848, the colonists occupied themselves by drawing up petitions and obtaining hundreds of signatures. Two petitions were completed in Cape Town – one sent to the Queen and the other to the Earl Grey. A third was sent from Grahamstown. Smith informed Grey that the people of the Colony would not abide the plan and should convicts be sent to Cape Town, the colonists would see to it that they would be abandoned on Robben Island.

Sir Harry Smith found himself in a difficult position. He could not defy an order from his superiors, but if the convicts were sent, it would cause his fall from grace in the Colony. On 8 February 1849 the *Neptune* sailed from England with 300 convicts on board. The convicts were taken to Bermuda and landed. Another 286 were taken aboard and the *Neptune* set her sails for the Cape of Good Hope. As the argument of the Colonial Office went, those on board were Irish peasants who had been driven to crime by famine and they were unlikely to repeat their crimes in a new environment.

Rumours in the Colony began to spread like wildfire. A ship was already on the water, packed full of convicts, and destined for the Cape! A resistance movement known as The Anti-Convict Committee (later Association) sprang up. Protest meetings were held. Prominent businessmen and politicians like John Fairbairn and J.B. Ebden became leaders of the movement and their influence reached as far as the British Houses of Parliament.

In the furthest corners of the Colony men were being urged to join up and sign the Pledge. It stated that any person that had anything to do with landing, supporting in any form, or offering employment to convicts from the *Neptune*, would be placed under a complete social and commercial ban by members of the anti-convict movement! This could and in some cases did mean ruin for a Cape merchant, unwary, humane or perhaps just plain greedy enough to assist the authorities with supplies for the convicts.

It is worth noting that Cape Town had not stirred a finger in the 60-year period during which 150 000 convicts had passed Table Bay on their way to Van Diemen's Land and New South Wales in Australia. Things had somewhat miraculously changed one September morning in 1849 when the 642-ton *Neptune* cast her anchor in the Bay.

The fire-alarm gongs were sounded, the church bells tolled and the infuriated populace turned en masse to watch the ship arrive – like a leper come unbidden and unwelcome at their door – with its cargo of 286 convicted criminals.

In June of the same year the ship *Hashemy* on arrival at Sydney harbour in Australia had faced a similar scene. The biggest anti-convict meeting ever was held. Thousands of citizens prevented the convicts from disembarking and called upon Governor Fitzroy to send his cargo of crimes back to England. Cape Town now faced a similar situation. Sir Harry Smith was filled with panic and he ordered that no one be allowed to disembark until clarification had been obtained from London. The *Neptune* lifted anchor, sailed around the Peninsula and waited off Simon's Town.

However, unknown to Cape residents, a momentous speech had been made in the House of Commons on the evening of 27 March 1849. After Benjamin Disraeli, leader of the opposition (and future Prime Minister), had sat down, Charles Bowyer Adderley, a 35 year old millionaire member for North Staffordshire, rose in support. 'I am the spokesman,' he said, 'for those who desire to see this great country act worthily of her great destiny as the parent of new nations whom she should rear at least to equal and not to disgrace their origin.'

Forcefully and with great oratory Mr Adderley thundered on in a damning attack on Earl Grey's policy to turn the Cape of Good Hope into a penal settlement. He declared: 'The noble Lord is quite satisfied that the convicts will not harm the Cape community, but what of the feelings of the Cape Colonists themselves, of what consequence are they? There are miles enough of ocean to dissipate their cries and strength enough to stifle them if needs be. But, if there be British blood enough in the colonies to rouse and animate resistance, I, for one, would not vote a shilling towards crushing a spirit, so becoming to their origin. Oh, that I could get half the indignation here that would be felt were a similar tyranny tried upon ourselves.'

When Mr Adderley resumed his seat, he had won his point. More than half the house supported him and the motion not to make the Cape a penal colony was carried. On February 13 the *Glentanner* arrived in Table Bay with a despatch ordering the *Neptune* on to Van Diemen's Land. The very next week she sailed for Hobart and the night of her departure was witness to the biggest celebration ever received by a ship in Table Bay. The town and suburbs of Cape Town were illuminated and massive fireworks displays lit the sky.

The members of the Anti-Convict Association assembled at the Commercial Hall and more than 160 people sat down to a celebratory dinner lasting well into the small hours of the morning. During the course of the long dinner no less than sixteen toasts were drunk, not least of all to the health of Mr Charles Bowyer Adderley!

During the following week it was proposed that the Heerengracht, the main street in Cape Town, be renamed in Adderley's honour. The motion was carried unanimously. In Grahamstown, Mr John Hunt, a master craftsman, produced an exquisitely carved solid stinkwood chair, which was presented to Mr Adderley in February 1851 in the name of the grateful inhabitants of the Eastern Province.

And that is how Adderley Street got its name. Whilst I fully agree that some name changes are necessary and useful in our new South Africa, I believe such decisions should be made only after a thorough investigation in which the history is carefully researched. This will prevent a councillor from proposing a name change for mere selfish political gain.

Entrepreneurs and liquor

S ome interesting and rather colourful people came out to this country in the wake of the two great discoveries of diamonds and gold. One of these was a young Hungarian Jew, Alois Hugho Nellmapius, who arrived in the Pilgrim's Rest area in 1873.

Nellmapius was a qualified mining engineer who put his expertise to good use in the area and became a very wealthy man. He ran a successful mule caravan service that traversed the tsetse fly-infested country between the town and Delagoa Bay. Its purpose was to provide a mail link to the port. More profitable for him and several others, of course, was the cheap contraband Portuguese liquor often carried to the goldfields on the heads of young Shangaan women, who on reaching Pilgrim's Rest would be sold into service as housekeepers.

Nellmapius soon saw business potential in spheres beyond the mining regions of Pilgrim's Rest. He became a successful farmer buying a large tract of land just south of Pretoria, which he named after his daughter, Irene. His successful career soon attracted the attention of important people in the Transvaal. He became a personal friend and confidant of President Paul Kruger. It was Nellmapius who mooted the idea to the President of granting concessions.

On 3 October 1881 the Volksraad granted A.H. Nellmapius the concession: 'For the sole right to manufacture from grain, potatoes and other products growable in the Transvaal, with the exception of tree fruits and grapes, and the right to sell in bulk and bottle free of licence such spirits'. It was given for a period of fifteen years, making Nellmapius the only legal licensed producer of spirits in the Transvaal for that period.

On 17 June 1882 Nellmapius ceded this concession to a partnership consisting of himself, cousins Isaac and Barnard Lewis, and Barnard's brother-in-law, one Samuel Marks. This capital laid the foundation for De Eerste Fabrieken. In June 1883 a very proud President Paul Kruger opened the new distillery and christened it Volkshoop – People's Hope.

Various lobbyists, like the mining magnates, wanted the black workers on the mines to spend their money on the purchase of liquor. If they did this it took them longer to save up to go home. Simultaneously, an anti-liquor lobby was formed, consisting mainly of local residents who were extremely concerned about the rise in crime resulting from the consumption of liquor.

Thus a 'great' liquor industry was born on a 4 000 acre site on the banks of the Pienaarsrivier, some ten miles east of Pretoria, on land that had formerly been Sammy Marks's farm, Hatherley. Here was constructed a reservoir with a capacity of 170 000 gallons of water; a plant for electricity generation; a four-storey central distillation plant; a boarding house for white workers; houses for married European employees and a suitably prestigious house for the distillery manager. But it was the three large grain stores, each with a capacity of 5 000 bags, that attracted the attention of the Transvaal burgers.

The entire operation could be viewed from the splendid residence belonging to Sammy Marks, the managing director. Lying some one and a half miles away and known as Swartkoppies, this grand house is today a national museum and is certainly worth a visit.

By 1889 the factory employed over 150 people and workers. It was producing 1 000 gallons of proof spirit from the grain supplied exclusively by the Transvaal burgers. There was a minor set back in mid-December that year when a fire broke out in the plant. The result was a two-month delay in production. The cause was believed to be arson and perhaps the work of illegal suppliers of liquor to the mine compounds.

Sammy Marks later decided that more capital was needed to expand the operation and he decided to go public. In November 1892 the concession holders exchanged money and shares in the old company for shares in the new Eerste Fabrieken Hatherley Distillery Limited. With the advantage of listing on the London Stock Exchange, the Hatherley Distillery was able to attract both national and international capital. The company was on the threshold of a period of spectacular expansion.

Seldom if ever, one must admit, have more ambitious plans for industrial expansion been launched in a safer and more sympathetic business environment! What more could capitalists ask for than a government-granted monopoly in a rapidly expanding market? And as the sole producer in the Transvaal of cheap spirits for African consumption, Hatherley Distillery in 1890 found itself a ready market of 14 000 black miners which had increased to 100 000 by 1899. This privileged access to the market was an important part of the Hatherley success story. It also marked the beginnings of large-scale liquor production in South Africa.

North to
the Karoo

O ne of my favourite places in South Africa is the Karoo. I am in awe of its vast, open, sparsely vegetated plains with air so clean that you can almost taste it, its harsh climate and stark beauty with incredible sunsets especially during the winter months.

This was the home of the Bushmen or San people and their ancestors. They have left a priceless heritage at places such as Driekops Eiland at Plooysberg where over 3 000 carvings are chipped into the Riet riverbed; and at Hopetown where some of the finest rock engravings or petraglyphs in the world can be found.

Not to mention the glaciated pavements, fossils and corbelled houses – I could go on and on. People should look afresh at the Karoo. It is not that dry, dusty place which you drive through as quickly as you can. It has a history stretching millions of years. It is almost a wonderland of things long lost, forgotten, and never learnt. It contains within it a mass of information that is truly awe-inspiring.

Millions of years ago, the shallow basin of the Karoo was a vast glacier that, on melting, became a huge lake. Eventually the water collected there burst through the escarpment and tore scars into the Swartberg Mountains, creating deep gorges like Meiring's Poort and mountain peaks 2 000 metres above the stream. Such was the immense scale of sculpturing that took place. After our hominid ancestors and then the Stone Age ancestors of the San, came the Free Burghers, wandering over the mountains against the wishes of the governors of the

Castle. The explorer, Ensign Isaq Schrijver of Leiden, was the first to describe a journey into the Karoo.

Schrijver was commissioned by Governor Simon van der Stel to lead an expedition to make contact with the powerful Khoekhoe chief of the Inqua. Van der Stel sent him on his way with 21 armed Europeans and two wagons loaded with strong liquor, tobacco, and red beads. Thus, 37 years after Van Riebeeck landed at the Cape, the first recorded expedition crossed over the Outeniqua Mountains and made its way into the little Karoo.

Schrijver's party located the Inqua chief very close to the present day town of Aberdeen, in an area of the country hitherto unexplored by the European settlers. On the way there he noted 'a plain, level as far as the eye could see'. Dr E. Mossop, who traced Schrijver's tracks, has shown that this was probably the portion of the Great Karoo east of the Blydeberg.

Schrijver finally crossed the end of the Swartberg range and spent several days bartering with the Inqua tribe at a place he called Vervallen Kastel, or 'ruined castle'. He turned around and driving along more than 500 head of cattle and a sizeable flock of sheep, headed back to Cape Town. The entire expedition lasted three months and, at the end, the redoubtable Schrijver wrote the following words: 'To God be thanks for his grace, that we have come hale and hearty through so many perils.'

It was only because of a dire shortage of meat that the governors of the Cape allowed the farmers to settle outside the boundaries of the settlement. They set up cattle farms in the loneliest places on earth and leading very isolated lives, they became a hardy and determined people with a restless spirit.

Isolation also bred resourcefulness. Some journeyed as far as the Cedarberg, cutting wood from the indigenous forests for their wagons and their homes. They tanned skins for veldskoene. They made bullets, not hesitating to melt down their precious cooking utensils when lead ran out. In a land without doctors, the women were the nurses, using salt, brandy, aloes, herbs and local balsams. When the grazing was depleted, people simply moved on.

There were no easy passes over the mountains in those days. To negotiate the steep inclines, the wagons had to be taken apart and everything lashed to pack-oxen. One can understand why the journey to Cape Town was undertaken only once every three to five years.

That is how Trekboer existence evolved. The Great Trek of the early nineteenth century was able to draw on experiences accumulated in the course of one and half centuries in the Karoo and beyond.

Of wars and 'witchcraft'

There is a missing element in the contemporary cries of criticism against colonialism and imperialism that I find difficult to understand. The Dutch have been slated, the British held accountable and yet nothing is ever said about the Germans. But the bloodshed that took place in German East Africa and in German South West Africa is beyond belief.

In South West Africa, it culminated in the trek of the Herero across the Magalagadi Desert in Botswana, which halted in the Phalala area of the Waterberg. The most serious war during the few decades of German rule in Africa was, however, the Maji-Maji Rebellion in German East Africa.

It is said that the uprising was the result of actions by traditional healers, demonstrating with doctored bullets how they could turn bullets into water. The rifle was fired and when the smoke cleared, the healer in question was seen standing with water running down his chest. However, I believe that it was the inherent cruelty to the local people that was the real cause of the massive uprising.

Dr Karl Peters, the Imperial Commissioner, was in plain terms, a murderer. He had instituted a reign of terror. It is on record that he hanged his servant for stealing cigars and, when his black mistress strayed, he had her sent to the gallows. Thank goodness that word of his crimes eventually reached Berlin and the man was dismissed!

General Von Liebert, the Governor of the colony, once declared: 'It is impossible in Africa to get on without cruelty.' And that is precisely the way many German officials behaved. Photographs of the time show brutal executions which remind one of the vivid images in Pippa Skotnes's brilliant book on the Bushmen, *Miscast*. East Africa was known as the 'flogging Colony' and the Germans as 'The people of 25' because officials administered a standard punishment of 25 lashes, with the aid of a mutilating rhino whip.

Some say that Africa is a land of the unexpected and a territory that appeared at any one time to be calm might actually be seething with revolt under the surface. This is what it was like with the Maji-Maji Rebellion. The Germans were taken by complete surprise.

The word Maji-Maji means water; and the term refers to the events in 1904 when a traditional healer in the Rufiji River valley distributed a 'magic' medicine which thousands of local people believed would turn German bullets into water and drive all Germans into the sea. This has a familiar ring to it like the cattle-killing in the Eastern Cape during the nineteenth century. It reminds one also of the Njami-Njami water spirit that lives at the base of the Victoria Falls.

During the early months of 1905 the African population of German East Africa, south of the Central Railway line, knew that the war drums would be sounding before the year was out. But still the Germans slept on. Count Van Gotzen, the Governor, said afterwards that the rebellion was the result of a widespread underground movement and that the Maji-Maji Rebellion was the last fling of an African paganism in revolt against Christian culture, represented in this case by Germany.

The murder of an isolated planter in the Kilwa district was followed by an attack on Liwale, where Bishop Spiers of the Benedictine Order, along with two brothers and two nuns, was massacred. Next came the murder of German traders, rubber planters and a police sergeant. Then Arab-owned stores and houses were looted and burnt to the ground. On one occasion Nyangao, a Benedictine convent near Lindi, was attacked. The inmates were expecting to be killed at any moment and were being given absolution by Father Leo as the rebels stood watching. Suddenly, as the priest stood up and made the sign of the cross, the rebels fled from

114

the mission and Father Leo was able to lead his party to the safety of Lindi.

The revolt continued to spread rapidly up and down the coast and across to Lake Tanganyika. Chiefs and traditional healers of the Wapogoro and Wagindo tribes became prominent leaders. Some 13 000 people simply ignored the German machine guns and inflicted heavy losses upon the garrison when they stormed Mahenge again and again. The rebels captured Kilosa and massacred the defenders. Even Dar-es-Salaam appeared to be in danger.

Nevertheless, a point was reached when the rebels noticed that the medicine was not working, but the healers had a ready explanation. If the dead did not rise immediately, they would do so within four weeks and would be stronger than ever before. The rebels were instructed to chant the magic words 'Maji-Maji' when they went to war.

It was recorded that when German soldiers heard the chanting of these words, their blood ran cold. Two cruisers were sent out from Germany with a contingent of marines from Germany's colonies, together with a number of Zulu men. Punitive measures began in October 1905 and lasted well into 1907 when the last of the rebels were rounded up.

The repression that followed was harsh. Permission was given to askari soldiers to loot and destroy every rebel village. Crops were burnt and one rupee was paid for every rebel head delivered. Thousands were killed and the famine and disease that followed resulted in the death of more than 200 000 people. It is said that some tribes never recovered and the Wagindo people were reduced to a mere remnant, much like the Herero from South West Africa on another occasion.

Let us heed the words of a journalist, C.G. Grey, who once said: 'History is the greatest plagiarist in literature and repeats itself to the extent that, if one knew all history, one would never make a mistake in life. One would know all of the mistakes that could be made. Those who would rather learn from bitter experience than from history have no need to read this stuff.'

Reflections on the Anglo-Boer War

As South Africans celebrate the centenary of the Anglo-Boer war and as one of the biggest superpowers, the USA, prepares to enter a most formidable war, it may be an appropriate time to reflect on what we have or have not learnt from a war fought 100 years ago.

At that time the Boers were going into the guerrilla phase of the war and the so-called 'Bittereinde' generals, Louis Botha, Smuts, De la Rey, Beyers and a few others had taken to the veld. The British under the leadership of Lord Kitchener had already taken Bloemfontein, the capital of the Orange Free State, captured Johannesburg with its gold mining wealth intact and had marched on to take the capital of the Transvaal, Pretoria. Anyone could see that the battle was lost.

On the Boer side there had never been more than 87 000 men in the field at any one point. All were volunteers. On joining their commando, they brought with them their own horses, saddles, rifles and ammunition, along with sufficient food for about five days. They received no pay from the time they joined until the time they went home.

On the British side things were quite different. There were 450 000 trained soldiers in the field. They were supplied with horses, saddles, rifles and ammunitions and generally enjoyed three meals a day. In addition, they received regular payment.

If your country has fallen and you were facing such immense odds, the question that demands an answer is – should you continue to fight?

The question became even more pertinent when Kitchener passed the notorious proclamation to the following effect: 'Because Boer wives living on the farms were giving sustenance to their men in the veldt, farms will henceforth be destroyed; and people, both black and white, will be placed in camps.'

As a nation we are now only too aware of the ghastly and tragic facts of that war which cost the lives of over 50 000 white and black South Africans. The scars in our psyche still run deep. There are many today that look back and regard the 'Bittereinde' Generals as heroes. One wonders if the generals realised the terrible consequences of their deliberate decision to carry on fighting. A decision that could not change the inevitable outcome of that war! The Boers still lost.

The reason for the defiance probably lies somewhere deep in Boer nationalism and in the concomitant hatred for British rule. The Boer cause was nicely summed up in the now very famous utterance of a young captive: 'You British people fight to die, we Boer people, we fight to live!'

Let's hope that as we stand on the precipice of yet another war, we may have learnt some lessons from our planet's war-torn history. Or will we commit the same mistakes over again?

Table Bay and its treasures

Somebody said long long ago while studying charts of the sea, 'These charts – I think the fairies have the making of them, for they bewitch even sober-minded men'. It was Sir Walter Raleigh who spoke these words; and never was a truer thing said. From time immemorial man has been drawn to the sea and the treasures it holds.

Our own Table Bay off Cape Town is literally littered with wrecks. From the sandy beaches of Bloubergstrand to rocky Camps Bay, lie the remains of Portuguese caravels, Dutch and English East Indiamen, galleons, schooners, steamers and liners. And Chinese porcelain almost paves several areas of the seabed.

Table Bay dredgers usually dig up these fragments of forgotten treasures. As they move tons of sand, they bring up shapeless masses of barnacles, sometimes containing a corroded Mauser rifle with the trigger mechanism intact, brass candle snuffers, quaint old bottles and hundreds of cannon balls.

Amongst the valuable artefacts found have been handsome George IV silver coins in almost mint condition and gold 'spade' guineas of George III that made the dredger crew on board stop in their tracks and wonder what treasure chest they had just passed over.

John Lethbridge from Devon in England was the first professional salvor to dive on these wrecks. The Dutch East India Company (VOC) brought him to the Cape in 1727. Finding this field of enterprise untouched in Table Bay, he proceeded to dive on the wrecks in the shallower waters. He made several rich hauls, including 200 bars of silver weighing 800 lbs and a chest of silver ducatoons with a salvage worth then of £20 000 – a fortune in today's terms.

Records of salvage diving off the Cape appear again only much later. In 1881 a Cape Town jeweller named John Cournenay employed an experienced harbour diver, Jan Steyn, to explore two famous wrecks. The *Haarlem* and *De Jonge Thomas* were both Dutch East India Company ships driven ashore by a north-westerly gale during the eighteenth century near the Salt River mouth. A primitive submarine eye was used to survey the seabed and two dark shapes were located and buoys placed to mark the location.

Jan Steyn went to work. First of all there emerged porcelain cups and saucers and then the real success, a large quantity of coins. The auction of these goods was advertised as follows: 'A lot of coins, some Chinese frivolities, a very curious bottle of Japanese-ware, and a conglomerate of rare China, iron, rust and sand. Items that would be of interest to the British Museum.'

There is no doubt that many more valuable items would have been salvaged on that occasion had a gale force wind not come up and washed the marker buoys away and a huge sea not broken into the bay from the north west, covering the wrecks with sand. The wrecks have never been seen since.

Shipwrecks were a common occurrence in Table Bay, particularly before 1860 when the breakwater was built by convict labour. As there was no protection until then, shipwrecks occurred every couple of weeks during the winter months. On those nights the bell in the Castle would ring, summoning Company servants for rescue. Near the beach stood the solitary gallows that was a grim reminder of the penalty for looting stranded cargo. On the night of 17 June 1722, for instance, there were ten wrecks. Some 660 lives were lost, together with cargoes of spices, tortoiseshell, sugar, saltpetre and silks to the value of £250 000.

Eighteen years later, the Dutch ship *De Visch* was observed drifting towards the shore, dragging her anchor. On board were twenty chests of gold and silver which were destined as pay for the Company's servants.

'I'll give two months' wages to every man who goes out to save that cargo,' shouted Governor Tulbagh in great desperation. And the result, of course, was that the whole cargo was saved!

There are still many money chests in Table Bay awaiting recovery and the archives are full of accounts of wrecks and the treasures that they hold. One such wreck was the *Huijs te Craijenstein* which ran onto the rocks off Camps Bay on a foggy night in 1698. Bars of metal bearing the Company's coat of arms have been recovered, confirming her identity. Near the same spot the Portuguese slave ship *San Jose* floundered, with 500 slaves in chains held in her hatches. The fortunate ones managed to remove their chains in time. But 200 drowned as the ship went down.

On 5 November 1799 a blood red sun rose and gave warning of terror to come. Remember the lines of the old saying of the sea:

A red sky in the morning is a Sailor's warning
A red sky at night, is a Shepherd's delight.

The Captain of the *Sceptre* ordered the striking of the topmast as the gale burst upon them with a roar. The ship's cables soon parted and she struck a reef. During that day many men were swept overboard and that night the entire poop deck was torn off with the men clinging to it for their very lives. Alas, as the survivors were nearing the shore, a great wave capsized the deck and all perished. There were 411 officers, men and marines on the vessel, and only 42 survived.

So when we stand and gaze out over the calm waters of Table Bay, it is well to remember the tumultuous and often bloody history of those waters. Its moods run deep in our country's history.

Tasmania's links with the Cape

A certain Captain William Bligh RN set sail from England on the HMS *Bounty*. His task was to transplant breadfruit trees from the island of Tahiti to the West Indies. And, as every schoolboy knows, that voyage ended in a famous mutiny and no breadfruit trees ever reached the West Indies.

However, what very few people know, even Tasmanians who justly claim their island to be 'the apple island of the world', is that Captain Bligh on that very same voyage succeeded in transplanting the first apple trees from the Cape of Good Hope to Tahiti. But Bligh, as a matter of fact, succeeded in doing even more. The story is a stirring one. It includes the epic journey of over 3 500 miles that Bligh made in an open boat, a feat of seamanship without equal.

Bligh set sail from Spithead, England, on 23 December 1787 and sighted the Cape on 22 May 1788. False Bay was the winter harbour and he took the *Bounty* around Cape Point to the anchorage, sheltered from the north-westerly gales, seaward of Noah's Ark rock. It gives one a strange feeling indeed to stand in the area today and visualise the *Bounty* out at anchor, in the company of seven other ships from Holland and France.

After arriving in Table Bay and saluting the Fort, the *Bounty* received the reply of an equal number of guns. Bligh went ashore to acquaint the Governor of his arrival and the *Bounty* sailed on to Simon's Town. It was a busy time as the ship was leaking badly and needed caulking. Bligh recorded that the Governor of the Cape, Van de Graaff, gave them a warm welcome and Lieutenant-Colonel Gordon was immensely helpful in procuring the seeds and plants that Bligh required.

Mutiny was far from the Captain's thoughts as he returned to Simon's Town and told the now infamous Fletcher Christian of his successful mission. It was especially useful that the *Bounty* had called at the time of the year when fruit trees and vines at the Cape were dormant and therefore easy to lift. In August the *Bounty* reached Van Diemen's Land, now called Tasmania. A landing was made at the mouth of a lagoon near Cape Fredrick Henry, which Bligh had visited eleven years previously with Captain Cook, aboard the *Resolution* and *Discovery*.

On the eastern side of the bay a plantation of rich loamy soil was prepared for some of the trees brought from the Cape of Good Hope. Bligh recorded the planting that took place: three apple trees, nine vines, six plantain trees, a number of orange and lemon seeds, cherry, plum, peach and apricot stones, pumpkin and two sorts of Indian corn, as well as apple and pear kernels. And for full measure, onions, cabbages and potatoes were planted near to where the *Bounty*'s water supply was replenished.

Bligh then sailed past New Zealand to reach Tahiti in 52 days. The log registered 27 086 miles from England, making an average speed of 108 miles a day.

Throughout the 24 weeks at Tahiti, Bligh's diary recorded the work of the zealous 'farmers'. No fewer than 1 015 breadfruit trees were transplanted into pots, which came to occupy all the available space on the decks. In addition, Bligh had planted a variety of orange and pineapple plants, vines and fig trees, all from the Cape of Good Hope. Thus, the plants that Lieutenant-Colonel Gordon had helped to secure for Bligh made history on Tahiti as the first of their kind.

Captain Bligh's utter absorption in agricultural pursuits during the five months at Tahiti gave the mutineers ample opportunity to plot their callous scheme and on Monday, 27 April 1789, off the island of Kotoo, the master's mate, Fletcher Christian, and the master-at-arms rudely awakened the Captain.

We all know the story. Captain Bligh and his officers were put off the *Bounty* onto a smaller open boat and their epic journey commenced. It was only on 12 June 1789 that they spied the island of Timor. The gruelling journey of 3 608 miles in an open boat was at last over!

Suffice is to say that, unknown to many of us, the trees taken from the fairest Cape played an important part in the unfolding of that epic adventure.

The story of the Orange River

S ome 1 600 kilometres away from its numerous sources deep in
the Maluti Mountains, flows the Orange River, bringing with it
old secrets, mysteries and legends and untold treasures. Having
wound its way across this incredible distance, so creating South Africa's
largest river, it eventually breaks through the sand bar and flows out into
the south Atlantic. Where the sea and the Orange River meet, lie the
memories of sterling adventures, of riches lost and found, and of escape
and death.

That meeting place of the river and sea holds an early memory of
Bartholomeu Dias. In 1487 he left a store-ship anchored there with a
crew of eight and on his return some months later, all but one of the crew
had disappeared. It is recorded that this sole survivor, literally, died of
joy at the sight of his comrades. The ill-fated sailors had no inkling that,
just below their feet, lay hordes of diamonds. Some 290 years later,
Lieutenant-Colonel R.J. Gordon, the famous explorer, having stumbled
upon the river, named it the Orange, in honour of the Dutch ruler, the
Prince of Orange.

Much later Sir James Alexander, who worked the copper mines up
river, established a little trading store on this same spot, also blissfully
unaware of the enormous wealth below his feet. It is to this man,
incidentally, that we trace the origin of the later name given to the spot,
Alexander Bay. Later still, Fred Cornell, one of the most famous
prospectors in South African history, decided to follow up the rumours

and myths about the presence of diamonds in the river. He risked life and limb prospecting for diamonds all along that river, but he also missed the Aladdin's Cave at Alexander Bay, by a few hundred metres. Such was the cruel fate of most prospectors in our land!

Instead, a freak of nature placed the fortune in the hands of a certain Dr Hans Merensky in January 1927, and within a few weeks later he was a very rich man. Thus, for 640 years, from the first recorded visit by Dias in 1487 until 1927, the river had managed to clutch this prize to its breast.

Shortly after the discovery, the State stepped in with barbed wire fences, guns and searchlights. There was almost a revolution amongst the desperate hordes of men who hurried from every corner in South Africa to make their fortune. Some of the diamonds that were found in the area were so superb, the stones so pure and beautiful, that they looked as if they had been already cut.

And so illicit diamond-buying began; a traffic, I believe, that will continue until there are no more diamonds in the ground. In fact, at one time, so many illicit gems were being thrown at the markets of Amsterdam and Antwerp that the control of the world diamond trade was under severe threat. Men in the state diggings tried every which way to smuggle out diamonds. They swallowed them and even inserted them into cuts in their skin. Still to this day human ingenuity surpasses all efforts at detection and parcels of diamonds leave South Africa on their way to London, New York and Amsterdam where it is not a crime to have uncut diamonds in one's possession.

People say that millions of years ago there were extensive pipes of diamond-bearing kimberlite, of which today's mines at Venetia, Jwaneng, Premier and Orapa are remnants. The pipes were eroded and over millions of years, the stones made their way down the gentle slopes into rivers and were washed down to the West Coast.

I also know of a prominent man in Durban who claims that by studying the rings of fossilised trees, he has discovered the ancient course of the Orange River, which apparently flowed into the Atlantic much further south than is the case today. If his theory is correct, then, hidden under the soil inland from the sea, in the ancient riverbed, lies a fortune of diamonds, just waiting to be unearthed.

We cannot leave the story of the Orange River diamonds without mentioning the river's mythical creature. Very much like the Nyami-Nyami of the Victoria Falls, the Orange River has a snake god that is said to live in a bottomless pit at the base of the Augrabies Falls in the swirling pools of the King George Cataract. The Falls, situated 120 kilometres from Upington, are actually higher than the Victoria Falls and as the Augrabies myth recounts, it is the hole at the bottom of the Falls that is the origin of all the diamonds in the area.

South Africa's longest river and one of its most important, boasts a proud new name. The Orange is today known as the Gariep, its original Nama name. Besides its association with diamonds, the Gariep has a myriad of still-unexplored stories to share with us.

James Pratt and the turn of destiny's tide

If one delves into the early records of Johannesburg and if they are correct – and I have no reason to doubt them – you will come across the name of a certain James Pratt. To most people today, the name means nothing. Pratt was one of the earliest settlers in the Witwatersrand area and this is the story of the part he played in the development of the City of Gold.

James Pratt was born the son of a Northumberland magistrate in the year 1831. A bank crash took care of the family's fortunes and James was forced to seek employment. He joined the British East India Company and whilst out in the East, he contracted a disease that resulted in the loss of his voice. He was sent to the Cape to recover his health and, like so many others before and after him, he fell in love with South Africa.

He enlisted in the British army and saw active service in the Crimean War, participating in the famous battle of Sebastapol, where he lost two fingers. After recuperating he returned to work for the East India Company until it was liquidated in 1858. He was compensated handsomely, but managed to spend quite a bit of the money in a very short space of time. It was then that he remembered the Fairest Cape.

He came out to South Africa and after a time, decided to go North into the vast unknown. Prior to leaving, he met an old prospector. Marais had recently returned from the Zuid-Afrikaansche Republiek, where he had fossicked around the area but had discovered nothing of value, despite having traversed the area of the Witwatersrand. He advised Pratt that if he was going north, he should purchase land as near as possible to the sources of the Limpopo River.

This turned out to be excellent advice, for one of the known sources of the Limpopo was the stream near the Parkview Golf Course, right bang in the middle of Johannesburg. Pratt purchased a triangle of land with two rivers forming the sides and the base formed by the hills of the Witwatersrand. It was an area of some 16 000 acres in extent, for which he paid the princely sum of £250! He planned to hold on to the land and slowly sell it off as the country developed. He had absolutely no idea of what he had just purchased!

This stretch of land today would cover almost the entire city of Johannesburg and be worth uncountable billions of rands! Unfortunately, fate plays its hand in varying ways.

There was trouble boiling in the Transvaal Republic. The Pedi, under Sekhukhune, were giving the burgers a tough time on the northern frontier. Theophilus Shepstone had annexed the Republic without a single shot being fired, under what I believe were false pretences, and the Boers were planning a rebellion against British rule. Cetshwayo was threatening to invade a portion of land lying between Natal and the Transvaal, or so the British maintained. Tempers began to flare on many sides and General Thesiger, afterwards Lord Chelmsford, called for volunteers. Pratt enlisted and saw active service in the Anglo-Zulu war of 1879. It was there that the might of the great Zulu nation was brought under the heel of the British boot and Zululand became British territory.

President Kruger and his associates were aware of the events being planned and they called upon all the burgers and farmers in the Transvaal to join the Transvaal Commando. James Pratt, staunchly British, was required by the President to take up arms against his fellow countrymen. He wrote back to Kruger saying, and I quote: 'I have always been an Englishman, an Englishman I shall die and I shall be on their side marching to Pretoria.' Pratt actually went even further than this. He raised a volunteer band and actively fought against the Boers. Not a very bright thing to do, especially if you owned such a vast amount of property in the Transvaal.

After the battle of Majuba, the British were forced to sue for peace and the Transvaal was returned to the Boers. The Boers had not, however, forgotten Pratt's actions during the war. They confiscated all his land and drummed him out of the Transvaal.

From then on things took a decided turn for the worse for Pratt. He became sickly and was forced to return to England where he ended up living in squalor at the Guildford Union Workhouse near London. Shortly after suffering a stroke, James Pratt, the one time owner of between 16 000 to 17 000 acres of prime Johannesburg real estate, worth an untold fortune, slipped his earthly bonds, and was buried in a pauper's grave.

There was, I believe, a very strange aspect to the conclusion of this story. When Pratt was still alive and in his seventies, Mr Hill, the Master of the Guildford Union Workhouse, received an enquiry about Pratt's particulars. Mr Hill forwarded them to the officer concerned in Ladysmith, South Africa. Unfortunately, the officer had already died in the relief of Ladysmith and that was where the matter was left. However, the enquiry had concerned Pratt's vast landholdings, which, had it been followed through, might have meant that with the Boers' defeat this prime land would have been returned to old Mr Pratt.

How cruel fate can be! One wrong move and you lose the lot.

Witwatersrand gold

The story of the discovery of Witwatersrand gold reads like a fairy story, a fable you could say of riches yielded from the depths of the earth, in amounts that boggle the mind.

In 1853 Pieter Jacob Marais panned for and found gold in the Jukskei and Crocodile rivers, north of Johannesburg. He was the first official gold prospector in the South African Republic. How cruel was fate to Marais! He turned his gaze to the north and, in so doing, he turned his back on the territories where rich deposits of gold lay waiting. On reading his journals, you find that he devoted his main attention to riverbeds. Time and time again, he returned to the Jukskei and every time he did so he crossed the 'Ridge of White Waters' or the Witwatersrand. It is almost as if the Fates had decided against him.

In 1874 Henry Lewis was fossicking around in the hills of the Magaliesberg when he discovered gold in both alluvial and quartz forms on the farm Blaaubank, owned by an 1820 Settler named Jennings. In 1875 the Nil Desperandum Co-operative Quartz Mine Company was floated, credited with the distinction of being the first company to carry out exploitation near the Witwatersrand.

The South African Republic was keen to locate and develop goldfields. An inspector was appointed and two prospecting parties financed by the government. The men scoured the area, but to no avail. Nevertheless, such processes served to heighten awareness of the search for gold. Soon people everywhere were talking of the probable fortune their farms held.

After an interruption caused by the first Boer War, the search soon resumed. In 1881 J.B. Bantjies was prospecting at Kromdraai (or Mogale City to give it its new name), north of Krugersdorp. In 1885 payable gold was found on the farm of Stephanus Johannes Minnaar and in December of that year the farm was proclaimed a public digging. The rush was on and every manner of people started arriving, driven and fired by the God called Gold.

On a farm Wilgespruit nearby the Struben brothers stumbled on 'The Confidence Reef' and by December of 1885, a five-stamp battery had begun crushing. Still the giant, the mother of all gold, remained hidden. In late 1885 George Walker and George Harrison, two down-and-out prospectors, arrived on the Witwatersrand on their way to Barberton. The Strubens gave Walker employment and Harrison was contracted to build a house for the Oosthuizen family on the farm, Langlaagte.

History records that it was Harrison who in the course of construction of the house on Langlaagte found the Main Reef. It was he indeed who received the discoverer's claim. However, Walker, in his old age, claimed that he, and not Harrsion, had stumbled on the reef while taking a stroll one Sunday morning in February 1886. He recognised it as a conglomerate and found it to be rich in gold.

Whatever the truth, and most people tend to believe Harrison's version of events, neither of the men, nor indeed the Oosthuizens, became rich as a result of the discovery at Langlaagte. The true worth of the find was only established later.

Soon after this Bantjies traced the main reef to the farm Vogelstruisfontein, and Henry Norse, to Doornfontein. It was also found at Turfontein by Geldenhuis and by the Strubens in the Germiston area. The finds ignited the entire world as the true size of the discovery at last began to sink into people's minds.

From every conceivable corner of our globe, people come in their droves. They begged lifts on the transport wagons and then walked after leaving the rail head. They rode bicycles along the rough tracks and faced the danger of wild animals both by day and night, driven ever onwards by that deadly form of obsessive madness known as gold fever.

People from every walk of life came to that dusty shantytown – beggars, priests, prostitutes, cardsharps, entrepreneurs, financiers, peasant farmers, workers, fortune seekers, hoteliers, dance-hall girls. They came from the Barberton area where the gold was running out and business was not all that brisk. Whiskey-sellers, traders, mechanics and miners flowed into the area and together they built the city of Johannesburg.

Having read about the origins of the city, it is not difficult to understand why Johannesburgers to this day live on the knife edge. Being conscious of the possibility of change at any time, they also have the biggest of all hearts in times of disaster. A sense of joie de vivre pumps deep in their veins. Like many of their ancestors, they know what it was like to be wealthy one day and down and out the next.

By September 1886, just months after the discovery of Langlaagte, a total of nine farms had been proclaimed public diggings. All the way from Germiston to Roodepoort lay priceless tracts of land, which, until a few months previously, were open treeless plains, only good for cattle. The names are legendary – Driefontein, Rietfontein, Elandsfontein, Turffontein, Randjeslaagte, Langlaagte, Paardekraal, Vogelstruisfontein and Roodepoort.

Once mining began many sorts of trades followed in its wake. Bars, brothels, shoemakers, saddlers, seamstresses, sirens and songsters were all in demand, as the town leapt into life. Work and play were plentiful. The new town of Johannesburg founded on the farm, Randjeslaagte, burgeoned. Large-scale industries followed in the area that was destined to become the modern, financial hub of our entire country.

This was the El Dorado that had been dreamed. Along with the influx of people came entrepreneurs and capitalists like Joseph Robinson, William Knight, George Goch, Barney Barnato, Cecil John Rhodes and Charles Rudd and local lads like Colonel Ignatius Ferreira and Messrs Wemmer, Wolhuter, Fox and Rimer. Much of the early capital on the Rand originated from the diamond fields of Kimberley.

The latter half of 1886 and first half of 1887 saw a massive scramble for gold-bearing farms, which changed hands at unbelievable prices mostly in cash and shares. The farmers of the area, very conservative in upbringing, referred to the new society as the Sodom and Gomorrah of the highveld. In these developing tensions were to lie the origins of a deep distrust between two very distinct cultures that would flare up into a conflagration in the not too distant future.

The first company to be formed was the Witwatersrand Gold Mining Company. It was established by William Knight and was registered in Kimberley in September 1886. By the end of 1887 there were no fewer than 68 companies with a nominal capital of over £3 million.

Another early starter was the Wemmer Gold Mining Company that by February 1888 was paying an 82,5% dividend a year! The Company's £1 shares were valued at £8 and the party seemed as if would go on forever! The gold mines were literally spewing out wealth and millionaires rose from the hot, dry highveld dust overnight.

Then came a whispering, from one mineworker to another, and then a rumble. The mines were going deeper and deeper and the nature and composition of the ore was changing. Iron pyrites had begun to appear and it gobbled up the mercury used in the extraction process of the gold.

The news of the problem spread like a highveld fire running before a strong wind and within a couple of days, the share market prices had plummeted. People lost their entire fortunes overnight and others were plunged into debt. Wave after wave of financial terror gripped the community and the realisation dawned that the glorious El Dorado had come to an end, like every other gold rush the world had experienced.

Fleeings and suicides became common as people who were worth a fortune the day before were unable to obtain one penny's credit in town. Shops and all manner of business closed down. Speculators left to seek fortunes elsewhere as the boom turned into a crash.

There are always some people, for whatever reason, who see beyond the panic. When everybody else believed that there was no way around the problem, these men had the chutzpah to buy the worthless shares in companies that could no longer extract gold. Believing in an imminent solution, they took the risk. The rest fled the scene in their droves.

When all seemed totally lost, a team of Scottish chemists came forward with a process of gold extraction by means of cyanide known as the MacArthur-Forrest process. It was introduced on the Robinson Mine in 1890 and by the end of the following year all the other mines had adopted this new, revolutionary process. Johannesburg rose like a phoenix from the ashes. South African gold production doubled from 1889 to 1891. By 1897 the Transvaal was producing 27% of the total world's gold production.

From these social and economic processes emerged the Randlords, a very wealthy group of people who had persisted and not run. They had the guts, perhaps even madness, to believe that the situation would come right. They were the ones who really made it big! And the nice thing is that there is a lot of their blood floating around in the veins of the people in our country to this day.

This is my take on things. It's not the time now to turn our backs and run away from our lovely land for, perhaps all that is happening, is that the cycle of history is about to repeat itself.

Able Seaman Just Nuisance RN

It was during the dark years of the World War 2 that these events took place. It is a story of a South African dog, who thought he was a sailor, and then became one.

The dog in question was a huge Great Dane owned by a certain Mr Chaney who worked in Simon's Town. The mostly British sailors at the Naval Base soon became very friendly with Nuisance and would take him for walks. In time they taught him to board the train and to accompany them during their escapades to Cape Town. Nuisance in turn grew to associate the British naval uniform with a friend and would attach himself to any sailor dressed in uniform.

At first and all too frequently, the railway officials would make a fuss and sometimes manage to push Nuisance off the train. No problem for the dog. He would disappear around the corner, wait for the train to pull away, come back and catch the next train! The rigid and parochially-minded railway officials became so enraged that they sent an official letter of complaint to Mr Chaney, warning that if the dog was not restrained, they would be forced to destroy it!

Then the Admiralty stepped in and Nuisance was made a full-time member of the British Navy. His official naval papers are worth a mention.

Surname:	NUISANCE
First Name:	JUST
Trade:	BONECRUNCHER

Religion:	SCROUNGER
Period volunteered for:	PERIOD OF PRESENT EMERGENCY

Able Seaman Just Nuisance was billeted or quartered at Simon's Town's Froggy Pond. His Commanding Officer was the well-known Commander C.B.O. Shakespear, who was once heard to remark that for the duration of his stay Just Nuisance was the only member of his staff who never saluted him!

The Royal Navy in Simon's Town had acquired a mascot and the Cape people an icon. He was issued with a brass tag that bore his name, rank and number, and the now legendary words 'South African Railways – Free Pass'. The population of Cape Town and surroundings came to know and idolise this canine hero. Everywhere you went, cab drivers, pub owners, grocers, houses of dubious entertainment and bus drivers, everyone, knew this gentle giant of a dog. The occasions when Just Nuisance went out with his mates and led those who had consumed one over the eight to Cape Town Station, accompanying them all the way back to Simon's Town, are too numerous to recount. He had a special seat on the last bus back to Froggy Pond and the days of his eviction from the train became a fading memory. It was noted too that no matter what, when 'God save the Queen' was played, Just Nuisance 'sat' to attention.

His fame spread far and wide and soon he was receiving mail, like the letter from Joan Steytler, and I quote:

Dear Nuisance,

I am having a Democratic Dog Show on Saturday afternoon, March 29th, at the above address, in aid of the Merchant Seamen's Fund. This is everybody's dog show, and prizes will be awarded for the longest noses, tails, legs, biggest spots, handsomest dog, ugliest dog, etc. There will also be a special Heitz Championship for the dog who shows traces of the most varied family tree.

I would be very honoured to have your very distinguished patronage, as I am sure it would add to the success of the show if I could print this on the entry forms....

Nuisance's reply was approved by the Commanding Officer – the only rating to have his personal mail opened and read by a Commander in the British Navy – and it went like this:

Dear Joan,

I thank you for your kind invitation in asking me to grace your show on the 29th Instant. I much regret, however, that, owing to the exigencies of the service, I shall be unable to attend.

My Commanding Officer informs me that my appearance might result in a flood of applications for my service with the Royal Navy, and, in view of the rise in the cost of living, an application to my Lords Commissioners of the Admiralty for an increase in the general mess rations at the present time would be unfavourably received.

To assist in the raising of funds for your excellent cause, I am prepared to loan you my certificate of service, which you could exhibit.

You know me
Nuisance

One of the more serious problems that Just Nuisance faced in being accepted as an Able Seaman in the Royal Navy was the fact that he was 'married' to a Great Dane called Judy, resident of the Prince Albert Hotel, Simon's Town. But, being a bit of a Romeo, and having an eye for the girls, he added a second string to his bow. He married another of his breed, Adinda, of Hout Bay, on 1 June 1941. According to his naval documentation, this made him a bigamist, as it states on his record that he married Judy on 25 August 1939. Judy was alive and no divorce had been granted! At least he lived up to the reputation that a sailor has a girl in every port!

On 7 August 1941 Adinda produced two puppies, Victor and Wilhelmina, and it was decided that they would be taken to Cape Town to meet their famous father and then auctioned off to the highest bidder, the proceeds destined for the war effort.

The pups arrived at Cape Town Station on 25 October to a tumultuous welcome. Nuisance, brought from Simon's Town, arrived in a lorry bedecked with a Union Jack and naval ratings as his escorts. The puppies were officially welcomed by the Mayor and Mayoress of Cape Town. Carpets had been laid for canine feet to walk upon and flags and streamers had been tied the length and breadth of Adderley Street. Cheering crowds lined the pavements and the entourage was taken to the City Hall. A Mr Jack Stubbs purchased Wilhelmina and Lady Robinson bought Victor, with hundreds of Pounds so accrued going towards the War fund.

What is amazing is that it takes a time of crisis like a war to bring to the surface people's finest qualities, such as loving and caring.

Simon's Town will never forget its famous dog. On 1 April 1944, on his seventh birthday, Able Seaman Just Nuisance RN passed away. At 11h30 on Saturday, 2 April, he was buried with full naval honours at Klaver Camp Cemetery near Simon's Town. Nuisance's body was wrapped in a Royal Navy white ensign and, as he was lowered into his grave, a bugler played 'The Last Post' and a party fired a volley overhead. More than 100 officers and ratings filed past, their eyes brimming with tears, and an entire nation mourned its loss.

Deserted towns – Steynsdorp

A s you drive eastward from the cities of the Highveld region towards the edge of the plateau, lying in front of you are the majestic mountains of Swaziland, which boast some of the oldest rocks on the planet Earth. In these beautiful, big, blue mountains are hidden many untold secrets and stories, slowly fading with the passage of time. The deep shadows hold only the faintest memories of adventures and adventurers of a time long gone by.

Listen to this story from these high Swazi mountain peaks and deep valleys of a town that grew, lived and then died – leaving nothing behind, but a few scattered piles of rubble lying in the long grass.

Along the beautiful Umholondosi River that winds its way through a lovely valley, we find Jim Painter and Frank Austin one day, panning for gold. In this most isolated of places, they strike it rich and, around the campfire that night, in a scene not difficult to visualise, they drink to the health of the town they know will surely follow. For no news on Earth spreads quite like that of a gold strike.

This was July of 1885 and by April 1886, the Mining Commissioner, David McKay Wilson, came down from Duiwels Kantoor – now called Kaapse Hoop – to ascertain whether the field was payable or not. By that time there were already 800 men fossicking around in that valley. They gave the town the name of Painters Camp and envisaged a shopping area as a central base. All sorts of tents and shacks sprang up, made of baked bricks, canvas and packing cases, with boundaries often demarcated in empty Square Faced Gin bottles.

McKay Wilson renamed the camp Steynsburg in honour of Commandant J.P. Steyn who had accompanied him there. It was later changed to Steynsdorp to avoid postal confusion with Steynsburg in the Eastern Cape.

The goldfield was known as New Paarl Field and a fair amount of gold was recovered from numerous reefs. Along with it, a bawdy community began formation. Liquor was consumed in huge quantities. And at night numerous tent fires would light up one side of the mountain as someone celebrated a find. Yet, close by, all was quiet as another prospector, lying in his bed of dried grass, wondered where his next meal would come from and yet another lay shivering from a bout of fever which haunted that town like the grim reaper.

On 21 February 1887 the town was finally declared a public digging and E. von Brandis was appointed mining commissioner. A Diggers' Committee was elected to run the town. The town was surveyed and grew at a phenomenal rate. The famous reefs, Ingwenya, Nevada, Southern Cross, Unity, Comstock and hundreds of others, yielded up their riches. The alluvial creeks, alone, like Fullerton Creek and others, attracted about 3 000 diggers to the area.

The town consisted mainly of canteens and grog shops, each with its own flag flying gaily outside. There were some 30 canteens in Steynsdorp along with a couple of hotels. Hotels like Duprats Royal Hotel were really 'like it or lump it' places, where the only comfortable bed was occupied by the owner. Here it was that the rough diggers gambled and fought, roistered and had their fun.

The stores were also memorable, each with its standard stock; preserved milk, bootlaces, castor oil, dynamite and fuses, carbolic soap, Cape brandy and, of course, Square Faced Gin. Digging implements lined the walls that were adorned in places with cuttings of beautiful women extracted from magazines. On the stamped earth and manure floors were stacks of mielie meal, sugar, flour and oranges.

An additional sign of 'civilisation' was the newly constructed goal, headed by a German called Gustav Milhorat and his wife Lizzie, a former well-known Barberton barmaid.

Jim Zulu worked for this pair and evidently harboured a deep grudge against them, for, at 23h00 on the night of 9 January 1889, Jim Zulu knocked on his master's door, with murderous intentions. On opening the door Milhorat was confronted with Jim holding a bayonet. Milhorat was stabbed eighteen times and his wife, who tried to intervene, received 22 wounds. They died in the doorway. The murderer was arrested and thrown into goal. Throughout the following day the diggers gathered in the canteens, discussing the possible repercussions that the event could have on the rest of the labourers, not least of all the Swazi warriors.

By 19h00 that evening, a force of 100 men had formed a lynch party. Down to the goal they marched, bundled the three guards out of the way and found Jim Zulu manacled in stocks and stark naked. He offered no resistance. They asked him why he had done it and he replied only, 'Me, Jim Zulu.' They threw a rope around his neck and frogmarched him down the road. Begemann, the local magistrate, ran into the road to intervene. They seized him, bound him with rope and left him at the side of the road. Up on the nek at the slaughter poles of the butcher Shultz, the mob hanged Jim Zulu and left him swinging there for the remainder of the night.

Some of the lynch party were later arrested and taken to Pretoria for trial. Frazer, D'almaine, Bachman, Solomon Rosenbloom and a few others but, we are told, they were eventually released through lack of evidence.

Such were the days of Steynsdorp. An excitable and temperamental population that revealed a mania for gossip and speculation, such as so and so's big find or Bill Jackson's bankruptcy. How much gold was actually recovered we will never really know, but one thing that we can say for certain is that there were more disappointments than rich men in the valley.

So, as the gold disappeared, the miners left one by one to try their luck elsewhere. The 'Bank of England' mine went bust. The 'Mint' went broke. The local newspaper, *The Observer*, found that circulation was falling and closed down. And little by little, the town fell to ruin. The few buildings that were left standing were looted and burnt by the ruffians of Steinacher's Horse during the Anglo-Boer War. Opportunist Swazis did the rest and at last there was nothing left.

Today just a few grass-covered mounds of crumbled brick remain as evidence of that once bustling little hamlet which had boasted a post office, Standard Bank, billiard saloon, music halls, stores, canteens, houses and the goal. And if you are ever travelling to Swaziland, you will find its remains just north of the Oshoek border post.

The early
Khoekhoe

For many years now I have been fascinated by the Native Americans, their numerous tribes, belief systems, social structures, dress and behavioural patterns, as well as the many festivals and dances celebrated by these often misunderstood people.

They perform Sun Dances, Moon Dances and Ghost Dances, dances for rain and fertility and, I presume, have a dance or festivity for almost anything imaginable. But what strikes me, most forcibly, is that right here, in our very own country, we have people and traditions as diverse and colourful as those of the Native Americans. They perform Spirit Dances, fertility rituals, Moon Dances as well as festivities to encourage the rainy season, the season of harvesting and the hunting season.

Why is it that some of us stand in awe of foreign cultures, but largely ignore our very own? It is a rather unfortunate fact that we do not realise what a great nation we are and what a diverse and rich history we have.

When you tell the average South African that the Magaliesberg are the second oldest mountains on the planet, you are greeted with a look of utter amazement, usually followed by the question 'Where's the oldest?' And the even more mind-boggling reply is, 'The Lebombo Mountains, also in South Africa.' When you tell people that The Cradle of Humankind outside of Johannesburg is where the very first forms of human life commenced on planet Earth, they are left gasping. But enough of that. Let's return to our people. Like the Zulu people, the Xhosa are composed of many different groups, such as the

Gqunukhwebe, Gcaleka, Pondo, Mfengu and numerous other small groupings. In this regard, the people who continue to intrigue me are those whom we were taught at school to call the 'Hottentots', but are today better known as the Khoekhoe.

Their dialects consisted of a series of complicated and delicate clicks using the palate and tongue, similar to what the Bushmen use still today. To the often uneducated Dutch and Europeans who came out to the Cape during the seventeenth century, anybody who spoke with a click and was not of a fair skin, was called 'Hottentot'. Nothing could be further from the truth. Let's go back to my original example. Amongst the Native Americans we find Cherokee, Seneca, Cheyenne, Pawnee, Comanche, Sioux, Cree, Mohawk, etc. And at home in South Africa, under the broad heading of Khoekhoe, we find the following historical groups of people. In an area starting from the northwest coast and Namaqualand, coming down towards the Cape of Good Hope and turning eastward to the Kei River, lived the Namaqua, Gurigriqua, Cochoqua, Goringhaikona, Gorachouqua, Goringhaiqua, Chamaqua, Hessequa, Attaqua and Inqua, etc.

These are just some of the tribes that populated our coastline and the interior of the Cape at the time of the arrival of the Dutch. The first three tribes we will look at occupied the area in and around Table and False Bay, as this is where the matrix of change and where disequilibrium were first experienced. They were the Goringhaiqua, whom the Dutch called 'Cape Men'; the Goringhaikona, called 'The Watermen' by the Dutch; and the Gorachouqua, whom the Dutch named 'The Tobacco Thieves'. But before going into specifics, let's look at some of the broader issues within the groups.

None of these people cultivated the soil. They were essentially pastoral people with herds of long-horned cattle and fat-tailed sheep. Their diet was principally milk, and women did the milking, whilst men performed general pasturing and herding activities. They supplemented their diet with wild fruits, berries and tubers of various kinds. Meat was a luxury and hunting was a task for the men. Domestic animals were never slaughtered, save on festive or ceremonial occasions. These nomadic tribes ranged in size from a couple of hundred to several thousand people and each tribe had its own territory. Land was exploited on equal terms by all sub-groups of the tribe.

An individual never owned land, nor did it belong to the Chief. Land was not perceived as alienable. In the old records of the Cape the several instances of land being 'sold' to the Colonists by Chiefs are not correct. Those transactions would have been looked upon as the granting of a usufruct. The so-called purchase price represented tribute paid for that usage. This vast difference in belief structure immediately set the stage for a conflict of interest. One people, for whom ownership of land was the basis of their culture, and another, for whom land could never be owned, but merely shared.

A second area of difference concerned tilling the soil. The Europeans regarded any unwillingness in this regard as pure laziness. However, according to traditional Khoekhoen cultural beliefs, cultivating the soil was prohibited. And here's the reason why. Everything was perceived as either male or female. The Earth was female and was akin to the female ova. When it rained, the millions of raindrops that fell on the land were like male sperm, penetrating the ova. With the help of the male Sun's warmth, which was likened to love, the female Earth would grow and people could live off the proceeds. For a man to interfere with these highly female and revered rituals of birth and growth would have been looked on with enormous disdain.

The Goringhaikona, Gorachouqua and Goringhaiqua were three of the Khoekhoe tribes that inhabited the area in and around Table Bay, Cape Point and False Bay. They were the first of many tribes to come into contact with the Europeans and the effects were to be devastating for them all.

The Goringhaikona were a small group of about 60 people, including women and children, who were also referred to in the records as the Strandlopers (Beachrangers). The tribe eked out a living by fishing and collecting creatures of the sea and they were noted as the only permanent inhabitants of the Peninsula at the time of the arrival of the Dutch settlers in 1652. They were the poorest of the three tribes and also supplemented their livelihood by selling their labour part-time to the settlers.

In the early years of contact with the Dutch this tribe was under the leadership of X'hore or Herry, as the Dutch called him. He was the well-known leader who had been taken to England long before the arrival of the Dutch, taught to speak English and returned to his people at the Cape. When the Dutch arrived at the Cape, they were met by X'hore who, to their utter amazement, greeted them in English. X'hore the Strandloper died in 1663 and was succeeded by Khaik Ana Makouka.

The Gorachouqua are now generally believed to be the ancestors of the Koranna. They adapted the name Koranna from the chief, Kora, and their tribal name, Koranna, thus means 'Men of Kora'. The tribe consisted of 300 to 400 men capable of bearing arms. Their Dutch nickname derives from the fact that the men once stole all the tobacco plants of a free farmer in the region. The area they occupied was east of Cape Town. They were pastoralists with long-horned cattle and fat-tailed sheep.

The Goringhaiqua were called 'Cape Men' by the Dutch because they occupied the lands where the Dutch had settled and because they always stated that the area was part of their ancestral lands. Their chief Gogosoa had two sons named Osinghaikanna and Otegnoa who constantly vied for chieftainship. The younger son constantly tried to do away with the elder. I quote from the records of Jan van Riebeeck: 'They are a bad lot, as they do not respect their chief.' They were a tribe of about 1 000 men.

In 1659, seven years after the Dutch settlement came into being, the first local war in the area broke out. The Goringhaiqua linked up with the Gorachouqua and attempted to expel the Dutch farmers from the area, stating clearly that this had been their land from time immemorial. They attacked the farmers, killing, burning and looting and successfully driving them away. A clever tactic they developed was to hold off the attack until it had started raining. The rain, of course, left the Dutch flintlocks utterly useless and, added to this, the Dutch were not very good at hand-to-hand combat.

One morning in June of 1659, after three months of skirmishes, a small group of Khoekhoe men were surrounded after driving off cattle. One of them, Eyakamma, who had been badly wounded, was taken back to the Fort for questioning. When asked why his people had attacked the Dutch and had caused damage by killing, plundering and burning, he replied in turn with a question. Why, he asked, had the Dutch ploughed over the lands of his people and sought to take food out of their mouths, by sowing corn on the very lands that were their traditional pasturage? The people had never had better, or indeed any other, grazing grounds. Eyakamma stated that the reason for the attacks was nothing more than revenge for the harm and injustice done to them. They had been commanded to keep away from certain grazing grounds, which till then they had possessed, undisturbed. Ever since they had permitted the Dutch to put up a victualling station, they had seen their lands being divided up without their consent and boundaries put up, which obstructed their pastoral activities. Eyakamma asked the Dutch what they would have done, had the same thing happened to them. He told them that he and his people had noticed that fortifications and bulwarks were growing on a daily basis. This, according to their way of thinking, could have no other objective than to bring his people and all that was theirs, under Dutch authority and domination.

Never were truer words spoken. When the Khoekhoe came to the Fort to sue for peace and press the land issue, this is what the Dutch replied: 'In consequence of the war you have waged against us, you have completely forfeited your right to the land and we will not restore it. The land now belongs to the Company by the sword and by the rights of war.'

Eyakamma was captured on 19 July and died in the Fort on Tuesday, 12 August 1659. This in a sense set the scene for South African conflict for years, if not centuries, to come.

Let us look at some of the now-extinct tribes that once inhabited the coastal regions. In the hills and valleys around Saldanha Bay there were the Cochoqua, or Saldanhars, as the Dutch called them. They were settled in fifteen or sixteen villages about a quarter of a mile apart. They possessed over 100 000 oxen and 200 000 sheep. Their facial features appeared finely chiselled and their hair was longer and less woolly than the other tribes.' Along with the Cochoqua lived the Little and the Great Charichuriqua. 'Chari' means 'small' and 'hurib', 'the sea'. The latter was a very interesting group of people. They quickly interbred with the whites and, as the pressure from farmers and settlers increased during the middle of the eighteenth century, they moved away to the north. They established themselves at Kamiesberg, in little Namaqualand, under the leadership of Adam Kok I. It was here that they were joined by various other groups of mixed Khoekhoe origins.

From the Kamiesberg they moved north again. This time to Pella, on the lower Orange River, north-west of present-day Poffadder. Here in 1813, they were encountered by the missionary, John Campbell, who managed to persuade them to resume their old, but now almost-forgotten name. They became known as the Grikwa and Grikwastad was named after them. Under a succession of able leaders, they played an important role in the political history in the making of South Africa.

In the other direction, eastwards from the Peninsula, far past the Attaqua and Auteniqua, dwelt what was said to be a savage race of people, who were dark in colour with hair so long that it flowed down their backs and hung on the ground. They were described as cannibals. They were called the Chabona. The Khoekhoe were terrified of these people, so it was related. It is apparent from Van Riebeeck's dispatches that the Chabona were not 'Hottentots' at all. The Chabona were what the Khoekhoe called the Xhosa. Van Riebeeck heard of this people from the now famous Khoekhoe girl, Eva. It was Eva who told the Dutch the marvellous tale of an emperor or king called Chobona, who lived far inland in a country rich in gold. She told them that the gold was taken from the sand and that the coins that were made were bigger than the palm of a grown man's hand. The people lived in large houses made of stone and beams, sowed rice and grew vegetables and spoke a language unlike any heard by the Hottentots in the Cape.

Jan van Riebeeck, haunted by the thought of their vast wealth, sent out several expeditions in search of these people, but could find no gold, nor locate Chobona.

The next group is the Sonqua who dwelt in the mountainous regions of the country. They numbered several thousand and were very small in stature, keeping no cattle and subsisting mainly on bulbs as well as hyrax or dassies. These people are of course the Bushmen or San who occupied vast areas in the central regions and the Drakensberg at that time. Suffice to say that the Bushmen gained a bad name amongst the Khoekhoe, as well as the settlers, for they believed that not only did the land belong to everyone, but the animals as well. The latter on occasions included cattle and sheep belonging to the Khoekhoe and the farmers. It has been said that this belief sometimes contributed to the Bushmen being hunted down and exterminated mercilessly by the farmers to the very brink of extinction.

The final group I would like to talk about are the Namaqua. Eva mentioned these people to Commander Jan van Riebeeck in 1657, but the Dutch did not come into contact with them until the Cruythoff expedition of 1661. In later years the Dutch learnt to differentiate between the Little Namaqua, living in what became known as Namaqualand, and the Greater Namaqua, living north of the Orange River. When first encountered, the Namaqua welcomed the Dutch with open arms. A group of about 100 musicians, each with a hollow reed of different lengths, stood in a circle and blowing on these reeds, produced a very pleasant harmony. The performance lasted for two hours and the Chief then entertained his guests with roasted lamb and milk. In return, the members of the expedition presented the Chief with copper, red beads, brandy and tobacco. These people had never smoked, nor drunk brandy. But this they learnt to do in a very short time and, as among the Inuits of Greenland, the custom was destined to become a scourge.

Before concluding this fascinating subject of the Khoekhoe people, I should like to make further mention of Eva. She was the niece of the famous Chief Herry and the sister-in-law of the Cochoqua chief, Oedasoa. Her real name was Krotoa. She was taken into service by the Van Riebeeck family soon after their arrival at the Cape and was so good at the Dutch language that she soon became employed as an interpreter. In 1657 she was fifteen years old. She was baptised Eva after the arrival of Commander Wagenaer in 1662 and in June 1664 she married the Company's explorer, Pieter van Meerhoff. She bore him three children. When he died in Madagascar, she slipped into a life of debauchery and was banished to Robben Island. She was later allowed to return to Cape Town and died on 29 July 1674. The official diary entry for the following day reads as follows: 'The body of the deceased Hottentoo, Eva, was, notwithstanding her un-Christian life, buried today according to Christian usage, in the Church grounds of the New Castle.'

I think that the traditional account of Eva's life is rather prejudiced for later research has shown that Eva actually accumulated wealth and property in Cape Town and was an accepted member of Cape society, but such are the biases that have been inserted into our history.

The
Waratah

N o shipwreck story has ever captured the imagination of the world as the *Mari Celeste* did. She was found in 1872, under full sail, near the islands of the Azores. Tables were discovered set, food had been prepared, halliards and sheets had been cleated, but not one living soul was on board the vessel. It was a spectacle that almost drove the Captain and the crew who boarded the strange ship to the brink of insanity. How could a crew simply disappear? No evidence of struggle, no looting and there were no lifeboats missing to account for disembarkation, a complete sailing vessel with no crew! It must have been a mind-bending experience indeed.

No less eerie was the experience of the *Waratah* off the East coast of our own country. I do not believe, incidentally, that we will ever see another vessel named the *Waratah*. Let me explain why. The barque, *Waratah*, was lost off Ushant, with thirteen lives on 16 February 1864, whilst sailing for Australia via Cape Town. On 2 June 1864 a schooner, also named the *Waratah*, left Newcastle, Australia, bound for Sydney. A huge northeasterly was encountered and she was never seen again.

In June of 1887 a 268-tonne steamer ran aground at Bullie, just south of Sydney. Her name was the *Waratah*. In January of 1894 a 203-tonne barque was driven ashore in the Gulf of Carpentoria. Yes, you guessed it – its name was the *Waratah*. And then on 26 July 1909 the 10 000-tonne *Waratah*, flagship of the Blue Anchor Line, left Durban harbour with 211 people on board, including 92 passengers.

She had set sail from Adelaide on 7 July and reached Durban on 25 July. There were 212 people aboard, but Mr George Sawyer, a commercial traveller from London who had joined the *Waratah* in Australia, thought the vessel was top-heavy as she had pitched and rolled excessively. This must have played on his mind for, the night before sailing from Durban, he had a strange dream. An apparition, in full matador's dress, carrying a sword, appeared to him and told him to leave the ship. He related this to his friends and they merely laughed. He was so disturbed by this dream that he went down to the ship's offices in West Street, Durban and arranged a transfer to another ship, cabling his wife to explain why he would be delayed.

Lucky man!

That evening the All-ashore bells of the *Waratah* rang and hasty good-byes were exchanged. The departure time had been brought forward as a result of the deteriorating weather conditions and for fear that the narrow exit over the harbour sandbar would be hazardous. Mr and Mrs W. Grant Dalton were seeing off seven members of their family. The ship's band played. There were the usual cheers and shouts and long streamers were thrown from the ship to the quay, as the *Waratah* slowly slipped away under the able guidance of Captain Trim, the tug master of the *Sir David Hunter*.

Trim's duty was to collect the harbour pilot, Captain Lindsay, from aboard the *Waratah* once Lindsay had cleared the harbour. Before handing over the *Waratah* to its own master, the famous Captain Illberry, the two captains shared a farewell drink; and then Lindsay departed. Their farewell handshake was to be the last human contact with the *Waratah*. When back in the tug, Captain Lindsay happened to remark to Captain Trim that he did not think that the *Waratah* was built for heavy seas and Captain Trim agreed.

The following day the *Waratah* overtook the *Clan MacIntyre* off Port St. Johns, the latter signalling 'Pleasant Voyage' with her flags. Only one other ship passed the *Waratah*. This was the *Guelph,* sailing from Cape Town to Durban, whose crew spotted the ship at 22h00 on Tuesday night, about 25 kilometres distant from the Bashee River, between Port St. Johns and East London.

152

On the following day, Wednesday, one of those unbelievable hurricane winds struck the area, known for this reason as the Wild Coast. But the *Waratah* was a well-equipped ship and was expected to ride out the storm, better than any others in the vicinity.

That Wednesday night, our Mr. Sawyer, in Durban, had another nightmare, in which he saw the *Waratah* in huge seas. A mountain of a wave struck her bows and she rolled to starboard, listing more, and more. Then she disappeared from sight. The following day he recounted this to his friends.

But an even more eerie event took place on the *Clan MacIntyre*, where the Chief Officer, C.G. Phillips, had relieved Captain Weir on the bridge. He sighted a strange old-fashioned sailing ship riding the storm and could not believe his eyes. She was sailing along, quite serenely, in the very teeth of the gale! This officer rose in his profession to become Commodore of the Clan Lines and so was no superstitious young mariner. He knew what he had seen. It was 'The Flying Dutchman' of Van der Decken, sailing to the scene of the tragedy. He reported the incident and the dates tallied with the *Waratah*'s movements.

The *Waratah* was never again seen and, in the search that ensued, ships from Durban, Cape Town and Australia covered thousands of nautical miles in a vain search. They did not find a single piece of flotsam. And although the wreck has recently been located, what actually happened that night remains a mystery until this day.

The life of
Margaretha Pietersen

Uring the early 1900s on the farm Helpmekaar, in the district of
Uitenhage in the Cape Province, lived the Pietersen family.
Gideon Pietersen was a tall blonde farmer of Dutch origins and
his wife Margaretha was of Huguenot descent, whose female ancestors,
since arrival in Africa in 1685, had all been voluntary midwives.

The year was 1918. Their eight-year old daughter, Charlotte, told her
father that the deaths the previous night had not been that heavy. Four
people, she continued, had died, two fewer than the night before. It was
the year of the great influenza epidemic and the Tembu people,
distinguished by their traditional vivid red cloth and beads, were dying
in great numbers. Margaretha was performing the role of doctor and
nurse on their own farm as well as on the adjoining four farms, which
together comprised an area of some 6 000 acres.

Some time after this father and daughter arrived at a little mud hut,
they dismounted and entered. Bending over a farm labourer, they found
the tireless Margaretha. The son of the labourer was assisting her in
wrapping the man in a blanket. 'He died about half and hour ago,' she
said. 'We have work to do and Daniel will help you dig the graves. He
is the fourth one.' Her husband responded, 'You're looking tired. You
should get some rest.' 'A rest,' she protested. 'Whatever for? My people
are dying and they cry out for my assistance. I will go on working and,
besides, someone has to look after the sick and bury the dead.'

Nobody really knows just how many people died in the epidemic.

Mrs Pietersen made a list of those they buried, which she sent to the local Justice of the Peace. And later, when she in turn became J.P., she kept the records. She spared neither herself nor her daughter. They nursed all day and most times far into the night, riding from place to place, administering pills and herb potions to the delirious patients.

An even worse epidemic in which Mrs Pietersen became involved, with heart and soul, was the outbreak of bubonic plague in 1925. At 3h00 one morning she was awakened by crying outside the house. She went to investigate and found a man who told her that his whole family had suddenly become sick and he was afraid that they were all going to die. She woke her daughter and they set out on their horses. Occasionally a dark form plunged across the narrow track in front of them, with a low growl, but these were hardened farming folk and the odd leopard did not scare them. After examining the wife, Margaretha's worst fears were confirmed. She found the knobbly tell-tale signs in the woman's armpits and in her groin. Dr Byrne, the district surgeon, would have to be informed immediately and the area placed under quarantine.

The following day, after examining the patients, Dr Byrne was heard to remark, 'We're in for a bad time, everyone in the area must be quarantined or we will have a plague on our hands in no time. As you know, the disease is carried by fleas from infected rats, and spreads like wildfire. The best we can do, seeing that we have no hospital, is to segregate the sick ones as far as possible and then, when they have recovered or died, to burn down the hut. He said to Margaretha, ' I know how devoted you are to these people, but I cannot blame you if you now keep away. You have your family to consider. God knows we need somebody to nurse but I must tell you that the disease is fatal. On other farms where there are cases of the plague, the farmers won't have anything to do with the sick. They are just staying at home and, quite frankly, I cannot blame them.'

Margaretha Pietersen placed her hands on her hips and looked at the doctor squarely in the eyes. 'These are my people and I will not desert them in their time of greatest need. Charlotte and I will nurse them.' She turned to her daughter and said, 'God knows we have work to do. Go into the kitchen, get a jar of paraffin and rub it all over you, in your hair, and on every inch of your body. This will prevent the fleas from biting you and if the fleas don't bite, you won't become infected.'

The number of cases rose to over 70 and many of the people died. Dr Byrne himself fell victim, leaving the full responsibility of doctoring and burying to the 45-year old Mrs Pietersen. The night sky was often lit up with the glow of burning huts. The local people called her Noyeza, the Medicine Woman, as she and her daughter rode from household to household, heedless of the danger to which they were exposing themselves.

It was only when Margaretha turned 80 that her family was able to convince her to give up her vocation. By that time she had delivered over 3 000 babies. As Mrs Charlotte Searle, Margaretha's daughter became the Director of the South African College of Nursing and was the first South African nurse whose research led to the award of a Doctorate. Doctor Searle's monumental thesis, 'A socio-historical survey of the development of nursing in South Africa from 1652 to 1960', remains the only complete history of nursing in this country. And her mother, Margaretha Pietersen, or Noyeza, was truly our South African Lady of the Lamp. We salute you both.

Events in the life of an English officer and gentleman

T here were many interesting characters sent out to South Africa from foreign shores and some have played an important part in the formation of our country. Others have left lasting impressions, both good and bad. One man, I feel, has been wronged by history and on a certain level used as a scapegoat for the wrongs committed by others. The man in question is Colonel Anthony William Durnford.

We pick up his story in Pietermaritzburg where he was a Major in the Royal Engineers, placed in charge of a group of Natal Carbineers. He was given the task of pursuing Chief Langalibalele, the head of the Hlubi tribe, in the vicinity of the Natal Midlands.

Langalibalele had been instructed by the government of Natal to register his tribe's rifles with the authorities. He had ignored the order three times and Durnford and his men were sent to bring in the recalcitrant chief.

Langalibalele's spies had told him of this decision and, along with his cattle and his men, he hotfooted it to the safety of Basutoland. Major Durnford and his men headed up the Bushmen's River Pass in the Giant's Castle area of the Drakensberg. After a bit of a mix-up, they eventually linked up with another section, only to find Langalibalele and his men already at the pass. In the ensuing fight, Durnford's horse, his treasured Chieftain, lost its footing and both horse and rider tumbled down the side of the pass. Miraculously, both survived the fall, but Durnford's left shoulder and arm were severely broken, as a consequence of which his arm was rendered useless and he had to carry it in a sling for the rest of his years. In that fight five men were killed. All were buried in the pass where they fell, and today there stands a monument to the men in Pietermaritzburg Market Square.

A strong party under Captain Allison, another famous name in the history of Natal, was sent to Basutoland, where they managed to capture Langalibalele. The Chief was to be banished to Robben Island but instead was kept at De Oude Molen, outside Cape Town. The township, Langa, formed later in the vicinity, was named after him. As a result of this rebellion the Hlubi tribe was broken up, their lands were confiscated by the State and the people who survived were captured and parcelled out as itinerant labourers to the various frontier farmers in the Midlands district.

Durnford did not agree with the handling of the Hlubi and took exception specifically to the policies and procedures of Sir Theophilus Shepstone, the head of Native Affairs in the Colonial Government. It is at this juncture in his life that he became estranged from colonial society in Pietermaritzburg. He became a virtual social outcast, to the extent that somebody even went as far as poisoning his beloved dog, Prince.

Durnford and his wife were separated. He said it was because she spent money too freely, but it was rumoured that she had taken a lover in town. His very liberal attitude toward the black people of Natal distanced him from colonial society and drew him closer to that other well-known champion of the downtrodden, the Rev. John William Colenso, or Somtsue, as the locals called him. Colenso also disagreed fundamentally with what was happening and he was not shy in making his opinion well-known. As a result of the handling of the Langalibalele affair, Durnford broke off his lifelong friendship with Shepstone and never spoke to him again. He found the actions of the government, in general, and those of Shepstone, in particular, utterly despicable.

Durnford found solace in the arms of the Bishop of Natal's youngest daughter, Francis Sarah Colenso. The 50-year old Durnford became the lover of the eighteen- or nineteen-year old Francis. Francis saw Durnford as her knight in shining armour and loved and idolised the man until her dying day.

Later, in 1879, we find Durnford commanding the reserves at Middledrift, while Lord Chelmsford's centre column crossed the Buffalo River to begin the invasion and destruction of the Zulu empire. Durnford sent a message to Chelmsford stating that an attack by the Zulus on Natal was imminent and that he wished to move his men to a new and better position of defence. Here is the reply he received from the bungling Lord Chelmsford:

> Dear Durnford, unless you carry out the instructions I give you, it will be my unpleasant duty to remove you from your command and to substitute another officer.... You have simply received incorrect information and your change will make it impossible for me to carry out my plan of campaign. I trust you will understand this plain speaking and not give me further occasion to write in a style that is distasteful to me.

I do not wish to delve into the details of the battle of Isandlwana, but Durnford arrived with his trusted Natal Native Contingent and they participated in that terrible battle begun by the British to destroy the might of the Zulu Kingdom forever. However, Durnford acted like the true man and soldier that he was and died at the head of his men.

Francis was utterly devastated by the death of the man she loved. Some years later she wrote a book about their life together called *My Chief and I*, under the pseudonym of Atherstone Wilder. It is a book well worth reading. And near to where this brave man fell, there is a monument to all the men who perished on that fateful day. It reads as follows:

Not theirs to take the day,
But falling where they stood,

To stain the Earth with brave men's blood.
For England's sake and duty
Let neither praise nor blame be placed upon their epitaph,
But let it be simple like that, which marks Thermopylae
Go! Tell it in England, you that pass us by
That here, faithful to their charge
Her soldiers lie.

Durnford was not to blame for the British defeat that day. It was a great Zulu victory. And the rest was merely blame-placing and position-securing by those in high office. In time the British managed to undermine the Zulu Kingdom and the British Government took over, as had happened some years earlier with the Xhosa in the Eastern Cape.

The ancient locket

D uring the Presidency of Paul Kruger of the Zuid-Afrikaansche Republic and some time after gold was discovered in De Kaap valley in the Eastern Transvaal, a certain gentleman, by the name of David McKay Wilson, was appointed Government Mining Commissioner. It was a position he took over from Christian Joubert, a relation of the renowned General Piet Joubert.

It took Wilson and his family seventeen days to trek to the Government Offices at Duiwels Kantoor in the Pilgrim's Rest area. His office represented the forces of law and order in the area. He had personally to examine and measure every claim that had been pegged, collect the claim taxes, issue and renew all prospecting licences, as well as settle disputes arising amongst the miners and, believe me, there were plenty of these. As part of a prospecting licence the law required that the miner log in a diary, daily, every single thing, and any and every anomaly found. And herein lies a very strange story.

Much remains to be said concerning the belief that has fascinated many travellers and explorers in South Africa over so many, many years. I refer to the now confirmed fact that the gold-bearing areas of our country were familiar to our country's ancient peoples. Every now and then something crops up which adds to this knowledge that Europeans were not the discoverers of gold in the southern part of Africa. Almost everywhere you look in ancient writings, books and manuscripts, you come across mysterious references to ancient mines, places of immense weath, empires built on gold and African tribal leaders with diamond adornments, etc. If you look at some of the back issues of the *Optima* magazine, you will find reference to the fact that all the alluvial and surface diggings, prospected in the southern part of Africa, had been worked before.

In 1884 a young prospector named Paskin applied to Wilson at Duiwels Kantoor for the necessary permit to sink a shaft in a certain forest that was government property. He stated that he wanted to test a theory that he held regarding the source of the alluvial gold in the De Kaap valley. Wilson issued the necessary permit and a month later he mounted his horse to check on the progress being made. He arrived as Paskin was being hauled out of the shaft to the surface. The prospector was carrying in his hand a small object, which they took to be a gold nugget. Upon scraping it and removing its casing of alluvial cement they found not a nugget, but a small square gold locket. It opened on a rough hinge, much like modern ornaments. On one side of the lid was a piece of parchment, inscribed with unrecognisable characters. On the other side, beneath a piece of mica, was a lock of human hair. The outside of the case was engraved with certain figures, which were later identified as Masonic symbols. The curious relic was later lent to the Masonic Lodge at Barberton and exhibited to a large number of knowledgeable people.

The locket had been discovered six metres under the surface. How it got there, who placed it there and when, and for what reasons, are all questions I'm afraid we will probably never be able to answer. But one thing is definite. Mr David McKay Wilson was a highly respected member of the community, who carried an important position at that time. He had no reason to report on hoaxes and he wrote of this incident in his book that was published in 1901.

The last known person known to have owned the locket was a Mr Paskin of Johannesburg some time during the 1880s. I have tried to locate his descendants, but to no avail. With modern dating and molecular techniques, we would today be able to establish the age of the artefact and thereby shed some light on a very mysterious artefact.

Bibliography

Anderson K. *Heroes of South Africa.* Purnell and Sons, Johannesburg.

Aylward, A. 1878. *The Transvaal of Today.* W. Blackwood & Sons, London.

Balfour A.B. 1970. *Twelve hundred miles in a wagon.* Pioneer Head, Salisbury.

Becker, Peter. 1967. *The Path of Blood.* Longman, London.

Becker, Peter. 1969. *Hill of Destiny.* Longman, London.

Becker, Peter. 1970. *Rule of Fear.* Longman, London.

Beinart, Delius & Trapido. 1986. *Putting a plough to the ground.* Ravan Press, Johannesburg.

Bevan D. 1972. *Drums of the Birkenhead.* Purnell & Sons, Cape Town.

Blackburn, Douglas. 1908. *The Prinsloo of Prinsloosdorp.* Alston Rivers, London.

Binns, C.T. 1974. *The Warrior People.* Howard B. Timmins, Cape Town.

Bloomhill, Greta. 1962. *Witchcraft in Africa.* Howard B. Timmins, Cape Town.

Bulpin, Tom. V. 1952. *Shaka's Country.* Howard B. Timmins, Cape Town.

Bulpin, Tom. V. 1953. *The Golden Republic.* Howard B. Timmins, Cape Town.

Bulpin, Tom. V. 1954. *To the Shores of Natal.* Howard B. Timmins, Cape Town.

Bulpin, Tom. V. 1955. *Storms over the Transvaal.* Howard B. Timmins, Cape Town.

Bulpin, Tom. V. 1957. *Lost Trails of the Transvaal.* Howard B. Timmins, Cape Town.

Bulpin, Tom. V. 1957. *Islands in a Forgotten Sea.* Howard B. Timmins, Cape Town.

Bulpin, Tom. V. 1959. *Trail of the Copper King*. Howard B. Timmins, Cape Town.

Bulpin, Tom. V. 1966. *Natal and Zulu Country*. Books of Africa, Cape Town.

Bundy C. 1988. *The Rise and fall of South African Peasantry*. David Philip, Cape Town.

Burman J. 1971. *Disaster struck South Africa*. Struik, Cape Town.

Burton A.W. 1935. *Sparks from the Boarder Anvil*. David Philip, Cape Town.

Chapman J. 1971. *Travels in the interior of South Africa*. Balkema, Cape Town.

Carruthers, Vincent. 1990. *The Magaliesburg*. Protea Book House, Pretoria.

Churchill, Lord R. 1994. *Men, Mines & Animals in South Africa*. Books of Rhodesia, Bulawayo.

Cloete S. 1958. *The Mask*. Collins, London.

Cloete, Stuart. 1963. *Rags of Glory*. Collins, London.

Cloete, Stuart. 1969. *African Portraits*. Constantia Publications, Cape Town.

Coetzer J.P. [1960's]. *Tales of Veldt & Vlei*. Maskew Miller, Cape Town.

Colenso F. 1994. *My chief and I*. University of Natal Press, Pietermaritzburg.

Colenso J.W. 1982. *Bringing forth the Light*. University of Natal Press, Pietermaritzburg.

Conan Doyle, A. 1903. *The Great Boer War*. Thomas Nielson & Sons, London.

Cope, John. 1967. *The King of the Hottentots*. Howard B. Timmins, Cape Town.

Dapper, Ten Rhyne, De Gravenbrock. 1933, *The Early Cape Hottentots*. Van Riebeeck Society, Cape Town.

De Wet C.R. 1902. *Three years War*. A. Constable & Co., London.

Delegorge A. 1990. *Travels in South Africa*. Vol 1 & 2. University of Natal Press, Pietermaritzburg.

Duminy A, & Guest B. 1989. *Natal & Zululand from the earliest times*. University of Natal Press, Pietermaritzburg.

Fuller B. 1953. *Call back yesterday*. N.V. Drukkerij, Amsterdam.

Goldie F. 1963. *Lost City of the Kalahari*. Balkema, Cape Town.

Green, Lawrence G. 1932. *The Coast of Treasure*. Howard B. Timmins, Cape Town.

Green, Lawrence G. 1945. *Where Men Still Dream*. Howard B. Timmins, Cape Town.

Green, Lawrence G. 1949. *Land in the Afternoon*. Howard B. Timmins, Cape Town.

Green, Lawrence G. 1952. *Lords of the Last Frontier*. Howard B. Timmins, Cape Town.

Green, Lawrence G. 1959. *To the River's End*. Howard B. Timmins, Cape Town.

Green, Lawrence G. 1961. *The Great North Road*. Howard B. Timmins, Cape Town.

Green, Lawrence G. 1966. *Thunder on the Blaauberg*. Howard B. Timmins, Cape Town.

Guest H.M. 1902. *With Lord Methuen & the 1st Division*. H.M. Guest, Klerksdorp.

Guy J. 2001. *The view across the River*. David Philip, Cape Town.

Harrington, A.L. 1980. *Sir Harry Smith*. Tafelberg Publishers, Cape Town.

Isaacs, Nathaniel. 1971. *Travels and Adventures*. Killie Campbell, Durban.

Johnson, Frank. 1940. *Great Days*. Books of Rhodesia, Bulawayo.

Klein, Harry. 1951. *Land of the Silver Mists*. Howard B. Timmins, Cape Town.

Kruger, Rayne. 1959. *Goodbye Dolly Gray*. Cassell, London.

Lehman, Joseph. 1972. *The First Boer War*. Jonathan Cape, London.

Lowe, S. 1967. *The Hungry Veld*. Shuter & Shooter, Pietermaritzburg.

Mackeurtan, Graham. 1930. *Cradle Days of Natal*, Longman Green & Co. London.

Manfred, N.H. 1960. *Voortrekkers of South Africa*. Tafelberg Publishers, Cape Town.

Marais, Eugene. 1928. *Sketse uit die Lewe van Mens en Diere*. Nasionale Pers, Cape Town.

McNeile, Michael. 1958. *More True Stories from this Africa*. McAlan, Cape Town.

Mendelsohn R. 1991. *Sammy Marks*. David Philip, Cape Town.

Metrowich, Frank. 1953. *Assegai over the Hills*. Howard B. Timmins, Cape Town.

Metrowich F. 1956. *The Valiant but Once*. Standard Press, Cape Town.

Metrowich F. 1968. *Frontier Flames*. Books of Africa, Cape Town.

Metrowich, Frank. 1962. *Scotty Smith*. Books of Africa, Cape Town.

Millin S.G. 1951. *The peoples of South Africa.* CNA, Johannesburg.

Milne, Robin. 2000. *Anecdotes of the Anglo Boer War.* Covos Day, Johannesburg.

Morris, David. 1966. *The Washing of the Spears.* Sphere Books, London.

Morton, Henry. 1948. *In Search of South Africa.* Methuen & Co., London.

Mostert, Noel. 1992. *Frontiers.* Pimlico, Johannesburg.

Packenham, Thomas. 1982. *The Boer War.* Futura, London.

Plaatje, Solomon. 1973. *The Boer War Diary.* Macmillan, Johannesburg.

Pringle, Eric. 1963. *Mankazana.* Eric Pringle, East London.

Rosenthal, Eric. 1951. *The Hinges Creaked.* Howard B. Timmins, Cape Town.

Rosenthal, Eric. 1955. *Cutlass and Yard-arm.* Howard B. Timmins, Cape Town.

Rosenthal, Eric. 1958. *Other Men's Millions.* Howard B. Timmins, Cape Town.

Rosenthal, Eric. 1959. *Shovel and Sieve.* Howard B. Timmins, Cape Town.

Rosenthal, Eric. 1961. *Encyclopaedia of South Africa.* Frederick Warne, London.

Rosenthal, Eric. 1979. *Memories and Sketches.* AD Donker, London.

Russell, R. 1911. *Natal, the Land and its Story.* D. Dries & Sons, Pietermaritzburg.

Samuelson, R.C. 1974. *Long Long Ago.* T.W. Griggs, Durban.

Scoble, John & Abercrombie, H.R. 1900. *The Rise and Fall of Krugerism.* W. Heinemann, London.

Scully W.C. 1984. *Transkei Stories.* David Philip, Cape Town.

Scully W.C. [19--]. *Between Sun and Sand.* Juta & Co, Johannesburg.

Shapera I. 1953. *The Bantu speaking peoples of South Africa.* Maskew Miller, Cape Town.

Schapera I. 1930. *The Khoisan peoples of South Africa.* Routledge & Kegan Ltd, London.

Shaw C.S. 1990. *The Karkloof Hills.* Shuter & Shooter Pietermaritzburg.

Schoeman P.J. 1957. *Hunters of the desert land.* Howard Timmins, Cape Town.

Van Warmelo D. 1977. *On Commando.* A.D. Donker, Johannesburg.

Wannenbergh, Alf. *Forgotten Frontiers*. Howard B. Timmins, Cape Town.

Williams, Alpheos F. 1948. *Some Dreams Come True*. Howard B. Timmins, Cape Town.

Wilson, David M. 1901. *Behind the Scenes in the Transvaal*. Cassell, London.

Wulfson, Lionel. 1987. *Rustenburg at War*. L. Wulfson, Rustenburg.